A Faithful Record of the *Lisbon Maru* Incident

Translation with additional material
by Brian Finch
of the original Chinese Book
published by SoftRepublic (Hong Kong, 2007)

Proverse Hong Kong

2017

Royal Asiatic Society Hong Kong Studies Series

Royal Asiatic Society Hong Kong Studies series is designed to make widely available important contributions on the local history, culture and society of Hong Kong and the surrounding region. Generous support from the Sir Lindsay and Lady May Ride Memorial Fund makes it possible to publish a series of high-quality works that will be of lasting appeal and value to all, both scholars and informed general readers, who share a deeper interest in and enthusiasm for the area.

Titles in RAS Hong Kong Studies Series:

Reluctant Heroes. Rickshaw Pullers in Hong Kong and Canton 1874-1954 Fung Chi Ming
Resist to the End. Hong Kong 1941-1945 Charles Barman, Ray Barman (ed)
Scottish Mandarin. The Life and Times of Sir Reginald Johnston Shiona Airlie
Six Day War of 1899. Hong Kong in the Age of Imperialism Patrick Hase
Southern District Officer Reports. Islands and Villages in Rural Hong Kong John Strickland (ed)
The Lone Flag. Memoir of the British Consul in Macau during World War II John Reeves
Watching Over Hong Kong. Private Policing 1841-1941 Sheila Hamilton

A FAITHFUL RECORD OF THE *LISBON MARU* INCIDENT is a recent translation from an original Chinese publication covering an important chapter in Hong Kong's wartime history. It gives details of the *Lisbon Maru* Incident of 1942, seen through the eyes of the Chinese fishermen who rescued hundreds of British prisoners of war from Hong Kong, whose ship had been torpedoed. The Japanese had tried to keep them in the holds as the ship sank so that they would drown, and then shot at them as they tried to escape. These courageous fishermen not only prevented hundreds more deaths, they also hid three prisoners under the noses of the Japanese until they could be sent secretly on a journey across more than 1,000 miles of China to reach Chongqing, from where they could tell the world what had happened. The book also recounts the visit to Zhoushan in 2005 of one of the survivors of the sinking and his emotional reunion with those who saved him; as well as a visit to Hong Kong in the same year of the last few remaining fishermen who had taken part in the rescue.

The translator, BRIAN FINCH, was commissioned into the Middlesex Regiment in 1960 and served with one of the survivors of the *Lisbon Maru*, sparking a life-long interest. He saw active service in Malaysia (where he commanded a platoon of Iban head-hunters), and later on peacekeeping duties in Northern Ireland. Following an intensive course in Chinese in Hong Kong he had a posting to the Headquarters staff where at the height of the Cultural Revolution he studied the deployment of Chinese forces along the Hong Kong border.

Brian Finch later joined the Foreign and Commonwealth Office where he used his knowledge of Chinese in support of the negotiations over the future of Hong Kong.

His years in Hong Kong led to a close relationship with the *Lisbon Maru* Association of Hong Kong, and since learning the full story of the courageous Chinese fishermen of Zhoushan who rescued hundreds of British prisoners of war from Hong Kong, including many from the Middlesex Regiment, he has worked closely with the Association to help their work of educating others about the incident, and this inspired him to translate this book. In 2011 he undertook a 117-mile walk from the south coast to the north coast of Devon across Dartmoor and Exmoor to raise funds for the Association.

He has previously translated into English the Chinese language website of the Dongji Museum of History and Culture, which is mainly about the *Lisbon Maru* Incident, for posting on another website. This current volume is his first venture into full publication.

Brian has been a member of the Chartered Institute of Linguists (formerly the Institute of Linguists) since 1971. He now speaks Mandarin Chinese to near-native standard and can get by in Cantonese; he is often mistaken on the telephone for a native Chinese. He reads Chinese in both traditional and simplified characters and writes it with a Chinese word-processor. He is married, and his son, daughter, daughter-in-law and granddaughters all live in Hong Kong, which he regards as his second home. Brian is a member of the North Dartmoor Search and Rescue Team (part of Mountain Rescue England and Wales), sits on a number of local voluntary committees and in his spare time enjoys bridge and playing the piano.

A FAITHFUL RECORD

OF

THE *LISBON MARU* INCIDENT

The story of 1,816
forgotten Second World War soldiers
from Hong Kong
and fishermen of Zhoushan, Zhejiang Province

Translation
with additional material
by
Major (Ret'd) Brian Finch, MCIL

of the original Chinese Book
compiled by members of the
Lisbon Maru Association of Hong Kong
under the direction of the late
Nelson Mar BEM

published by SoftRepublic (Hong Kong, 2007)

Proverse Hong Kong

A Faithful Record of the *Lisbon Maru* Incident
Translation with additional material by Brian Finch
of 實錄里斯本丸事件, by Hong Kong *Lisbon Maru* Association,
first published in Hong Kong by SoftRepublic Ltd, 25 July 2007,
Sponsored by Lord Wilson Heritage Trust.

Translation rights in the original Chinese publication (實錄里斯本丸事件)
have been granted to the Translator by Lord Wilson Heritage Trust.
This translation, with additional material,
is published in Hong Kong by Proverse Hong Kong, 16 November 2017.
Copyright © Proverse Hong Kong, 16 November 2017.
ISBN 978-988-8228-87-4

Distribution (Hong Kong and worldwide):
The Chinese University Press of Hong Kong,
The Chinese University of Hong Kong, Shatin, New Territories, Hong Kong SAR.
E-mail: cup@cuhk.edu.hk. Web site: www.chineseupress.com
Tel: [INT+852] 3943-9800; Fax: [INT+852] 2603-7355.

Distribution (United Kingdom):
Enquiries and orders to Christine Penney,
Stratford-upon-Avon, Warwickshire CV37 6DN, England.
Email: chrisp@proversepublishing.com

Enquiries:
Proverse Hong Kong, P. O. Box 259, Tung Chung Post Office, Tung Chung,
Lantau Island, NT, Hong Kong SAR, China.
E-mail: proverse@netvigator.com Web site: www.proversepublishing.com

The right of Brian Finch to be identified as the author of this work has been asserted by
him in accordance with the Copyright, Designs and Patents Act 1988.

Printed in Hong Kong by Artist Hong Kong Company, Unit D3, G/F, Phase 3, Kwun
Tong Industrial Centre, 448-458 Kwun Tong Road, Kowloon, Hong Kong.
Cover image (The Sinking of the *Lisbon Maru*),
courtesy of the Council of the National Army Museum, London.
Translator portrait by Gillian Finch
Cover design by Raoul Solomon

British Library Cataloguing in Publication Data
A catalogue record for this book is available from the British Library.

This translation is dedicated to all who suffered on board and following the sinking of the *Lisbon Maru* and to the Chinese fishermen of Zhoushan who showed such extraordinary courage in rescuing hundreds of British prisoners of war.

Table of Contents[1]

Table of Illustrations[2]

Acknowledgements

I am most grateful to the following:

Simon Yao, Chairman of the *Lisbon Maru* Association of Hong Kong, and Kent Shum, Secretary of the Association, for their encouragement in the translation of this book, to Kent in particular for helping me to understand some of the more arcane Chinese expressions.

Lord Wilson Heritage Trust, which sponsored the publication of the original Chinese book, for giving permission for the publication of this translation.

The Sir Lindsay and Lady May Ride Memorial Fund for accepting this work as part of the Royal Asiatic Society Hong Kong Studies Series.

Tony Banham who corrected my misspellings of some of the non-Chinese names and pointed out a few historical inaccuracies in the original, which are recorded in notes; who supplied to the authors of the original Chinese book the list of names of those who died in the sinking of the *Lisbon Maru* and has agreed to its publication in this translation, and who also kindly wrote the Foreword.

Hugh Baker, Professor Emeritus of Chinese at the School of Oriental and African Studies, London, who kindly checked my work, correcting some issues not only with the Chinese translation, but also with my English, as well as making helpful suggestions about the general layout of the book.

Madoka Sato who helped with some of the Japanese names.

Elizabeth Ride who drew my attention to the account of the escape route taken by the three prisoners of war, which appears in the Appendices, and to the National Archives in Kew, Surrey, which kindly gave permission for its reproduction.

Richard Jordan (on behalf of the Jordan family) who supplied the images of his father Charles Jordan as a young man, details of his time in a prisoner-of-war camp and his life back home after the war, letters from Buckingham Palace and the US 8th Army HQ and for drawing my attention to his oral history held by the Imperial War Museum.

Finally I cannot express strongly enough my profound thanks to the vision, encouragement, help, advice and tireless efforts of Dr Gillian Bickley in supporting this work and in preparing it for publication. Without her support it is unlikely that it would have seen the light of day.

Any errors that remain are of course mine alone.

Illustrations and other permissions and acknowledgements

I am most grateful to the following individuals and organisations who helped in identifying or supplying the photographs or other images used in this book, or provided other information about them: Darryl L Baker; LCol (Ret'd) Ron Burch, Manager, Royal Winnipeg Rifles Museum; Barbara Davis of the Mare Island Museum; Toru Fukubayashi, Co-representative of POW Research Network Japan; Makoto (Mack) Horie, Vice Director, NYK (Nippon Yusen Kaisha) Maritime Museum; Richard Jordan, on behalf of the Jordan family; Paul Johnson, Library Manager, The National Archives Image Library; Dr Alastair Massie, the National Army Museum; Michael Mohl, Battleship and Submarine Archive Manager, navsource.org; Yuki Ogawa, Assistant Curator, NYK (Nippon Yusen Kaisha) Maritime Museum; Danielle Sellers, Deputy Curator, the Royal Engineers Museum; Kent Shum, Secretary of the *Lisbon Maru* Association of Hong Kong; Dawn Watkins, Picture Library Team, the National Army Museum; auto.eastday.com; Combined Fleet; Getty Images; HyperWar Foundation; Imperial War Museum; Naval History and Heritage Command, US Navy; www.flickr.com/photos/deckarudo/6302204318/.

I acknowledge with thanks the following individuals and organisations for permission given for the illustrations or other materials to be included as follows:
Getty Images (Sakai Takashi entering the city); Imperial War Museum, London (prisoners of war on the move, image of Charles Heather and Charles Jordan's oral history); Mare Island Museum (USS *Grouper* official photo); National Archives Image Library, Kew (the *Lisbon Maru* sinking); Council of the National Army Museum, London (the sinking of the *Lisbon Maru*); NYK

(Nippon Yusen Kaisha) Maritime Museum, Yokohama, Japan (the *Lisbon Maru* with flags); Royal Engineers Museum, Chatham (prisoners of war sent to Moji); SoftRepublic, from the public domain ("128 incident", Winnipeg Grenadiers, Japanese marines landing at Tsing Yi, prisoners of war disembarking, the *Lisbon Maru* under way, map of the tracks of the *Lisbon Maru* and the USS *Grouper*, the Dongji group of islands, the map of the track of the *Lisbon Maru* and the small picture of the USS *Grouper* in the Appendices); US Naval History and Heritage Command (USS *Grouper* port side view).

Kent Shum (on behalf of the *Lisbon Maru* Association of Hong Kong), gave permission for all other images not listed above.

If acknowledgement is missing to any person or organisation, this will be remedied in future editions if notification is received.

Foreword

The sinking of the *Lisbon Maru* was a human tragedy. More than 800 men lost their lives that day, and a further two hundred perished within the next two months of the combined effects of shock, exposure, malnutrition, exhaustion, and disease. Many more of them would be dead by war's end. But this was 1942, early in a war that would lead to more than sixty million deaths. By the time peace returned, the *Lisbon Maru* had been forgotten, swamped by deaths on an industrial scale from the eastern front to the concentration camps, from the bombing of cities to D-Day.

In 2005 I completed a book about the sinking. During its preparation I had the honour and privilege of speaking to many survivors. They graciously and generously told me their stories, happy that at last someone was showing an interest in their fates and those of their comrades. Now the majority of those men have passed away, but I was touched when so often I would receive letters from their families saying how much 'dad' had enjoyed working with me, and how he always kept a copy of that book on his mantelpiece.

Roll forward to 2015. At a State banquet in October, President Xi of The People's republic of China, sitting next to Queen Elizabeth II, rose from his seat and addressed the guests. In his speech, to my astonishment, he mentioned the *Lisbon Maru*. But well he might; it was an outstanding example of China's and Great Britain's wartime ties. Ordinary Chinese fishermen, already impoverished by years of war, had sailed out to sea under the noses of the Japanese and rescued several hundred drowning POWs. Bringing them to their islands, they gladly shared what little food they had.

These stories, and the ship that inspired them, are remembered once more; this new translation is proof of that.

Thanks to individuals in China, Hong Kong, and the UK (including Brian Finch, the translator of this work) the incident has been brought back to life. Today, this human tragedy – and the heroism it inspired – is no longer forgotten.

Tony Banham
Hong Kong, December 2015

Introduction

The *Lisbon Maru* Incident is a story of hardship, horror, tragedy and extraordinary courage. In 1942 the Japanese freighter, carrying British prisoners of war from Hong Kong to Japan, was torpedoed off the coast of China, near Zhoushan. The author Tony Banham, in his book *The Sinking of the "Lisbon Maru": Britain's Forgotten Wartime Tragedy* (published by Hong Kong University Press ISBN 962-209-771-5) has written a meticulously researched and detailed account which describes the atrocious conditions endured by the prisoners from the moment they got onto the ship, the horrors of being confined in the holds as the ship was sinking, and the cruelty of the Japanese as they opened fire on the prisoners who jumped from the ship to save their lives. The Japanese managed to transfer their own soldiers and crew to other ships which came to help, and could have transferred all the prisoners as well. Instead, they tried to ensure they all drowned.

Chinese fishermen from the local islands jumped into their flimsy fishing boats and at great personal risk went out time after time to rescue as many of the drowning prisoners as they could. Despite their efforts, 828 drowned and their remains still lie on the sea bed off the Chinese coast.

Readers are strongly recommended to read Tony Banham's book.

This book, written originally in Chinese, is a natural follow-up to Tony Banham's account. It came about as follows: In 2004 the authorities in Zhoushan began to plan for a ceremony to be held the following year, which marked the 60th Anniversary of the end of the Second World War (which the Chinese regard as The War of Resistance against Japan), to commemorate the part played by the fishermen in saving the lives of British prisoners of war following the sinking of the *Lisbon Maru*. Officials went to Hong Kong to try to find some survivors. They contacted the Second World War Veterans' Association in Hong Kong and were assisted by the Secretary, the late Nelson Mar, BEM. Mar was able to track down a former coastal gunner, Charles Jordan, who had survived the incident and was living in the UK. Jordan was duly invited to the ceremony in 2005 where he had an emotional reunion with the fishermen who had saved his life as well as the lives of hundreds of his comrades.

This experience spurred Mar to set up the *Lisbon Maru* Association of Hong Kong, with the aim of keeping alive the memory of the tragedy through publicity and other means and helping to support the surviving fishermen and their families. This book was written as a result of researches by Mar and other members of the Association.

Although the story is the same as that in Tony Banham's book, this account is viewed through the eyes of the Chinese taking part in the rescue, and includes eye-witness accounts from the fishermen and others involved, relatives of those who helped in the rescue, as well as material from Chinese archives not previously seen. It also covers in detail Charles Jordan's visit to Zhoushan in 2005 with a number of articles describing the emotional nature of that visit and the deep impression left on those who witnessed it. Seven of the fishermen paid a visit to Hong Kong in 2005 where they received a warm welcome and much praise from local organisations as well as the Hong Kong press.

During Jordan's visit to Zhoushan, the party was accompanied by several journalists and a group of young students from Hong Kong, who went there to learn history "by exposure" rather than from textbooks. Their touching accounts show that this was a successful exercise. As well as the universal admiration shown both for the frail and elderly Charles Jordan and the astonishing selfless courage of the Zhoushan fishermen, the students and the press draw the conclusion that it is important to understand and learn from the horrors of war so as to try to live in peace in the future.

The courage of the Zhoushan fishermen provides one of the finest examples of people-to-people co-operation between China and Britain. It should not be forgotten.

Brian Finch
November 2015

A Faithful Record
of
The *Lisbon Maru* Incident

Introduction by Nelson Mar, BEM
Chairman of the *Lisbon Maru* Association of Hong Kong[5]

Friends:

First, I am extremely thankful that we were able to get financial assistance from the Lord Wilson Heritage Trust, enabling us to publish this book, "A Faithful Record of the *Lisbon Maru* Incident".

Even now, many people still remember the iron heel of Japanese militarism: as well as trampling all over China, they did not exclude Hong Kong. We have many comrades who gave their precious lives performing their duty in the battle to defend Hong Kong in the merciless flames of war; and after the surrender, many comrades experienced years of extensive hardship in concentration camps and lost their youth suffering severe torment.

Can the allied prisoners of war who went through the murderous *Lisbon Maru* disaster and the heroic actions of the Zhoushan fishermen be forgotten after all this time? Hundreds of British prisoners of war were rescued by the fishermen at the time, thus narrowly avoiding disaster and surviving. The year before the disaster of the sinking took place, they were soldiers doing their utmost to defend Hong Kong and resist the Japanese invasion. After all this time, many compatriots have already gone quietly, and even those still in this world are old and frail, but the children of the next generation will be able to remember the kindness and generosity of the Zhoushan people. Under conditions of extreme wartime shortage of goods and materials, the prisoners who were rescued all received clothing and food.

Time passes quickly. China and Hong Kong have both changed considerably since the War; but the tragedy that took place in the Zhoushan archipelago in Zhejiang Province in 1942 must on no account be forgotten. 2007 is the 65th Anniversary of the *Lisbon Maru* disaster. The purpose of publishing this book, apart from reawakening the fond memories of our comrades, is also to enable us to review this incident, educate the new generation, cherish the present, look to the future, and make a contribution to the country and the nation.

Many young friends often ask me whether I came across any splendid stories during the war years. I always say to them: the majority of compatriots who were in fierce battles at the time were killed on the battlefield; we managed to stay alive because we were on the side-lines of the battles; war is always terrifyingly brutal like this; it always creates broken families, some gone away, some dead, the prime culprit for the scattering of one's family. We don't want war, what is needed is peace.

Today it is ten years since Hong Kong returned to the Motherland; in my lifetime I have seen the country grow prosperous and strong. Young friends do not need to face the threat of war again, making me think that the experiences of fighting the war for justice were all worthwhile.

Apart from the kind support of the Lord Wilson Heritage Trust, the smooth publication of this book also relied on Department Head Jiang Jianguo, Deputy Department Head Yang Xiao, Director Zhou Yongzhang, Madam Zhang Minfei and Mr Hong Xiaoming, all of the Zhoushan City Sinking of the *Lisbon Maru* Incident Research Society, supplying a large amount of valuable material and photographs. Apart from this, Mr Tony Banham, Mr Kent Shum, Mr Simon Yau, Mr Frank Lee and Mr Ian Parkinson of this Association and friends from all over (including Mr Ho Ming-sze, Mr Arthur Gomes, Mr Wong Chi-hon and Mr Charles Jordan) all made great efforts for the successful publication of this book.

Also, I should like to take this opportunity to offer special thanks to the late Mr Henry Fok, Vice Chairman of the Chinese Peoples' Political Consultative Conference, for making arrangements for a special dinner party for the elderly fishermen from Zhoushan when they visited Hong Kong, and meeting them in person.

Nelson Mar BEM
Chairman, *Lisbon Maru* Association of Hong Kong

Preface by Mr Arthur Gomes, MBE, Chairman of the Hong Kong Prisoners of War Association.[6]

Distinguished Guests, Ladies and Gentlemen.

By September 1942, those of us in the Hong Kong garrison who had fought to defend our homes, families, and friends, had already been prisoners of war for ten months. There was little food, but much disease. Many had died since our surrender.

When word came that some prisoners were to be shipped to Japan, some of us envied them. We thought that wherever they were going, they would be better off than we were starving in Shamshuipo Camp. We were wrong. Within days of the sailing of the *Lisbon Maru*, rumours started. We heard that the ship had been lost, and hundreds drowned. It was only after the war ended that we learned the truth of our comrades' suffering and also heard how so many had been saved by Chinese fishermen who had pulled them from the sea under the very noses of the Japanese.

Many of those survivors believed that without the courageous actions of these Chinese civilians, all would have been left to drown. Their intervention had averted a far larger disaster, and on behalf of all the Hong Kong Prisoners of World War Two, I would like to take this belated opportunity to give the fishermen and people of Zhoushan our personal and heartfelt thanks.

Speech of Mr. Arthur Gomes MBE (1917-2007)
Chairman, Hong Kong Prisoners of War Association

Contents[7]

The Full Story

of

The *Lisbon Maru* Incident

The incident of the sinking of the *Lisbon Maru*: 1,816[8] forgotten soldiers from Hong Kong.[9]

Drawn at Kobe concentration camp by British soldier WC Johnson[10]
who survived the sinking and was recaptured by the Japanese. The original
is now kept in the Regimental Museum of the British Middlesex Regiment.[11]

That day the sky was clear and the sea was calm. The *Lisbon Maru*, carrying nearly two thousand prisoners of war from the British army and 800 officers and soldiers of the Japanese army, was en route in the area of the Zhoushan archipelago, not far south of Shanghai. This cargo ship, full of allied prisoners of war, had not informed the International Red Cross Committee, nor was it flying any warning flag to show that there were prisoners of war on board the vessel. An American submarine, which just happened to be in that area carrying out patrol duties, fired torpedos at the cargo ship, after which the *Lisbon Maru* sank.

Originally, this kind of sea disaster would be really insignificant in the Second World War, in which there were tens of millions of casualties. However, this group had already made a contribution to the defence of Hong Kong, and having been made prisoners of war, had finally been sent to Japan to do hard labour. Therefore, so far as Hong Kong is concerned they are significant.

Ten months earlier in December 1941, these British imperial soldiers had played an important role in the 18-day battle that took place in Hong Kong. Who could imagine that that day they would die from being torpedoed by an allied submarine?

At the last moment, a group of local fishermen took to their crude fishing boats and rushed to the scene and one by one saved British prisoners of war who were on their last gasp struggling for their lives in the angry sea and took them to the nearby Qingbang[12] and Miaozihu Islands to recuperate. Reinforcements of Japanese gunboats caught up with them not long afterwards and forced the villagers to hand over the prisoners of war.

This then is the incident of the sinking of the *Lisbon Maru*. According to statistics, the ship was carrying a total of 1,816[13] prisoners of war from the British army. After the *Lisbon Maru* was sunk by torpedos fired from an American submarine, altogether 843[14] prisoners of war drowned at sea. According to the recollections of some of the survivors, when the *Lisbon Maru* sank, the Japanese soldiers closed the hatches and abandoned ship and fled, leaving the prisoners of war to be entombed,[15] and later opened fire and shot dead prisoners of war jumping for their lives into the sea. No-one would guess that unexpectedly, at the last moment, the fishermen who lived locally entered this historical arena and alleviated this tragedy of the war.

Historical background

The story can be told starting with Japan's aggressive ambitions against China. In 1931 (the sixth year of the Japanese Shõwa period), in the name of protecting Japanese railways, mining and other commercial interests, the Kwantung Army stationed in Manchuria decided to realise its wild dream of invading China, come what may. At the time, the local warlord Zhang Zuolin rejected the demands of Japan which hoped to establish a colony in Manchuria, and the Japanese army plotted to assassinate him. On 18 September, the Kwantung Army took the initiative and blew up the track on the Willow Lake section of the South Manchuria Railway line, in a place not far from Fengtian (present day Shenyang) and put the blame on the Chinese army, fabricating an excuse to invade. This was the so-called "9/18 Incident", also known as the "Shenyang Incident" (called by the Japanese the "Manchuria Incident").

After the "9/18 Incident", war erupted throughout China. The picture shows the Japanese Army in Shanghai fighting in co-operation with armoured troops from Jiangwan Garrison during the "128 Incident" or the "First Shanghai Incident" in 1932. At that time Japan, already one of the industrialised nations, had mobility superior to any army in Asia, and gained great superiority during the early part of the campaign to invade China.

The 9/18 Incident could be said to be the prelude to the Japanese invasion of China. For all sorts of reasons, the army in Manchuria, commanded by Zhang Zuolin's son, Zhang Xueliang, did not offer fierce resistance, resulting in the northeast part of China, known at the time as the "Hot River", quickly being declared as completely occupied and falling under the control of the Japanese Kwantung Army. On 1 March the following year, the establishment of "Manchuguo" was proclaimed, the puppet régime propped up by Japan, and Pu Yi[16] was appointed Head of State.

World opinion, led by the League of Nations, widely condemned Japan's invasion, but took no concrete action to prevent its brutal actions. The territory of Manchuguo is three or four times the area of Japan; with an area even greater than that of France and Germany combined, and provided a large amount of manpower and productive resources for Japan's plan to invade China.

This news of war, reaching the ever quiet and peaceful Hong Kong from faraway North China, did not immediately influence the colonial government's preparations for war. In fact, as early as 1922, it was stipulated in the Washington Treaty signed by the USA, the UK and Japan, that the main force naval tonnage of the three signatory nations was to be in the ratio 5:5:3, and at the same time the treaty clearly laid down that the UK was not to deploy military facilities within the limits of the Pacific Ocean east of Longitude $110°$, which indirectly affected the work of organising the defence of Hong Kong, situated to the east of this demarcation line. Only after Japan had swallowed up the vast territory of Manchuria and the interests of countries such as the UK and the USA in China had been threatened, did Hong Kong wake up from its state of long term torpor. The UK convened the London Navy Conference in 1933, and revoked the scope of the Washington Treaty, so that the UK could again plan the defence of Hong Kong.

British imperial officials believed that although Japan could defeat Chinese troops, they would not prevail so easily against crack British troops. Because of this attitude of treating the enemy lightly, the colonial government lacked a long-term comprehensive plan with respect to guarding against Japanese invasion.

Several years passed, and Beijing, Shanghai and Nanjing fell into enemy hands one after another and the Nationalist Government was forced to retreat to the provisional capital of Chongqing. London sensed that the possibility of Japan seizing Hong Kong was increasing daily and set about formulating a relatively comprehensive defence plan for Hong Kong. In July 1937 the Hong Kong British government passed an emergency ordinance announcing the maintenance of a neutral stance towards the Sino-Japanese War and prohibiting any ships coming from Hong Kong to assist any Chinese or Japanese ships. It was no doubt hoped that this policy would be able to draw a clear line with the closely approaching war, in the hope that Hong Kong would become an open city and avoid the flames of war.

The recently appointed Governor of Hong Kong, Sir Geoffrey Northcote, recommended simply abandoning the weak defences of Hong Kong; only the British prime minister, Churchill, insisted that Hong Kong should not be abandoned, pointing out, "Although Hong Kong cannot be held, it must be defended". That Spring, Hong Kong held the first large scale air defence exercise, and the government started to follow the defensive plan: air raid shelters, pillbox positions and anti-aircraft installations were built, and arrangements made for defensive lines all over Hong Kong Island, Kowloon and the New Territories.

However, in September 1939 Nazi Germany launched the *blitzkrieg*, sweeping across mainland Europe, and the UK itself suffered greatly from German air raids. It was in fact so tied up in looking after itself, that basically there was no way it could send more troops to defend a colony in the Far East. To strengthen Hong Kong's defence forces, in July of the same year the colonial government passed the "Compulsory Service Ordinance" stipulating that all qualified males of British nationality must serve in the armed forces.[17] This was the first time in history that the UK had introduced conscription in its colonies.

A Winnipeg Grenadiers group photograph before going to the Far East.[18]
The battle for the defence of Hong Kong led to one of the largest losses
of casualties and prisoners of war in Canadian military history.

In Summer 1941, Hitler launched a large-scale attack on the Soviet Union; and Japan, as one of the Axis powers, also quietly planned simultaneous attacks on British and American targets in many places in the Pacific Ocean, amongst which was Hong

Kong. Although the international situation was perilous with war looming, many military and civilian colonials continued to ignore Japanese ambitions, in the optimistic belief that the Japanese, whom Westerners always lampooned as "yellow-faced monkeys", would not be able to summon up the courage to challenge the military might of Britain and America.

The occupation of Hong Kong

Before the Second World War, it could be said that the British forces had never had any experience of fighting the Japanese forces. According to British military records, one incident of a clash between the two forces took place in 1937, during the period when Japan sent bombers to violently bomb cities in southern China: a British warship moored on the banks of the Yangtze River suspected it was mistakenly bombed by a Japanese aircraft. In 1938, Maj Gen AE Grasett, who was appointed Commander British Forces Hong Kong, [19] publicly stated that even though the Japanese could defeat Chinese troops, this certainly did not mean they could easily overcome crack British forces. This force commander's mindset of underestimating the enemy influenced to some extent the enthusiasm of senior and junior members of the forces, leading to undue slackness in the defence of the New Territories and other places.

In Gen Grasett's plan there were two important lines of defence in the New Territories: the first line started in the east at Sha Tau Kok, via Lo Wu along the Shum Chun River to Deep Bay in the West; the line was close to the China-Hong Kong border. The second was an unbroken line of over 70 miles, [20] the "Gindrinkers' Line", proclaimed by the British army to be impregnable. British army engineers built many pillboxes, machine-gun emplacements, trenches and tunnels. In parts of the construction the thickness of the concrete reached one and a half metres. Little wonder that the British army believed this defence line could withstand a Japanese army attack.

In fact, following developments in the situation in the European theatre, the British Empire had to transfer its sea, land and air forces from all over back home to resist the forces of Nazi

Germany. The strength of the regular infantry in the Hong Kong garrison did not reach four battalions. Furthermore, the empire's Far East Commander-in-Chief and Staff Headquarters had earlier been set up in Singapore, to the south, and not in Hong Kong. At that time the traditional strategy was that if Hong Kong were to come under a sudden attack, reinforcements could come from Singapore. Also, US naval and air forces stationed in Manila and Pearl Harbour could arrive very quickly, and it was therefore natural to put the centre of the defence in Singapore.

At the beginning of 1939, Hainan Island fell into Japanese hands and the reinforcement route was cut. Strategically, Hong Kong could be considered completely independent. Moreover, no-one had considered the Japanese military would risk everything and launch the Pacific War, simultaneously launching surprise attacks on many places such as Malaya, Pearl Harbour and Manila, setting alight many flames of war. It could be said that Hong Kong's desire for the assumed reinforcements to be sent from these places had come to absolutely nothing.

In August 1941 Maj Gen Grasett was sent back to General Staff Headquarters in London and was succeeded in the post of Joint Service Commander by the fifty-something-year-old Maj Gen CM Maltby. After Gen Maltby was appointed, he energetically reorganised the defence works, concentrating on setting up defence installations at the landing points around Hong Kong Island including anti-aircraft artillery and machine-gun positions. However, the war had reached the stage when Britain itself was already tied down coping with attacks by Nazi Germany and was basically too busy to take care of the defence of Hong Kong. Therefore Hong Kong's defence strategy was, that when attacked they would destroy the communications and oil depots etc. in the New Territories and Kowloon and all forces would withdraw to defend Hong Kong Island. They hoped they would be able to hold out for a number of months and wait for reinforcements.

Finally, on the morning of Monday 8 December 1941, war arrived. Some hours previously, the Japanese Combined Fleet had launched a surprise attack on US forces at the naval base in Pearl Harbour, and at daylight began attacks on British colonies such as Malaya and Hong Kong. Japanese forces in Guangzhou, which had been preparing for war for a long time, with the 38th Division as the main force, under the command of Sakai Takashi, Commander of the 23rd Army, first sent bombers to launch an air attack on Kai Tak airport, Kowloon, destroying the defending forces' only remaining five ancient and dilapidated military aircraft.

Troop strengths of British forces (joint British and Commonwealth forces) stationed in Hong Kong on 8 December 1941.

Royal Artillery 8th Coastal Regiment	537
Royal Artillery 12th Coastal Regiment	403
Royal Artillery 5 AA Regiment	588
Hong Kong and Singapore Royal Artillery 1st Hong Kong Regiment	874
Royal Artillery 965 Defence Battery	147
Royal Scots, 2nd Battalion	769
Middlesex 1st Battalion	764
Winnipeg Grenadiers	92
Royal Rifles of Canada	912
Hong Kong Volunteer Defence Corps	1,947
Royal Corps of Signals	1,759
Royal Army Ordnance Corps	132
Royal Army Service Corps	197
Royal Army Veterinary Corps	5
Royal Army Medical Corps	172
Royal Army Dental Corps	10
Royal Army Pay Corps	28
Rajputs 5th Battalion, 7th Regiment	892
Punjabis 2nd Battalion 14th Regiment	1,005
Royal Indian Army Service Corps	13
Hong Kong Mule Corps, RIASC	253
Indian Medical Service	60

The above makes a total of 11,559 officers and other ranks including staff serving in the Joint Headquarters.

The Commander of British Forces in Hong Kong, Maj Gen Maltby, commanded two battalions of British infantry, two battalions of Canadian infantry, two battalions of Indian troops, six companies of Hong Kong volunteers,[21] supported by the Royal Regiment of Artillery, the Hong Kong Singapore Artillery Regiment and the Royal Navy, altogether over fifteen thousand defending troops, opposing nearly thirty thousand invading Japanese troops. Because the Japanese forces had absolute air supremacy and were prepared for war, the defending troops, under attack by the highly motivated Japanese army, kept on retreating. Even the "Gindrinkers' Line", which the British Army thought it could defend for some time, fell within three days. All British forces hastily withdrew to defend Hong Kong Island and the whole of the Kowloon Peninsula fell into enemy hands.

The Hong Kong defence forces in traditional entrenched machine-gun positions were unable to resist the swift and fierce Japanese attack, supported by air raids by Japanese bombers, and finally surrendered after 18 days. The picture shows Japanese naval marines landing on Tsing Yi Island.

The isolated Hong Kong Island was faced with the crisis of food and water being cut off. The troops defending the island originally thought the Japanese would land from the west. They did not expect the Japanese army to choose to cross the sea at Lyemun in the east and successfully establish a beachhead, where a continuous stream of Japanese troops and equipment entered

Hong Kong Island from the eastern harbour. After the Japanese had landed they immediately occupied strategic facilities such as the electricity power station and the oil storage depot, and cut the fresh water supply on the island. The defending troops were forced to move their defensive line step by step to the south, finally engaging the invading Japanese forces in battle in places such as Wong Nai Chung in Happy Valley, Repulse Bay and Stanley.

The "Entering the City" ceremony held in Nathan Road, Kowloon, after the battle was over, led by Lt Gen Sakai Takashi, Commander of the 23rd Army stationed in Guangzhou, who commanded the Japanese forces' attack on Hong Kong. (The Asahi Shimbun Collection/Getty Images)

After numerous British soldiers had been killed, wounded or taken prisoner, Maj Gen Maltby considered the situation hopeless, and together with the Hong Kong Governor, Sir Mark Young, crossed Hong Kong Harbour on Christmas Day, went to the Japanese military headquarters in the Peninsular Hotel in Kowloon and signed a formal surrender document with the Japanese army, and Hong Kong officially fell into Japanese hands.

As for the Japanese, this was the first time they had successfully occupied by force an overseas colony of a European nation.

Concentration-camp life

Eighteen days of battle resulted in 2,133 casualties in the defending forces, and more than 8,500 were taken prisoner, including Canadian, Australian [22] and Chinese officers and soldiers. Most of these prisoners of war had been occupying defensive positions such as the Shing Mun redoubt, Wong Nai Chung, Repulse Bay, Mount Davis and Stanley and became prisoners of war after they were captured by the Japanese army. Initially, the Japanese had not made any plans to house prisoners of war. They drove most of the prisoners to Shamshuipo Camp. In the latter part of January 1942 around two thousand prisoners of war were transferred to North Point Concentration Camp, originally built by the Hong Kong Government to accommodate refugees, because Shamshuipo Camp was excessively overcrowded.

British Army and Canadian Army prisoners of war going to a concentration camp escorted by Japanese military police. Despite having become captives, British prisoners of war still maintained discipline when in concentration camps
(© Imperial War Museum (HU 2779))

At first the Japanese were somewhat lax in guarding the prisoners and therefore there were many incidents of prisoners escaping. Later they increased the number of guards, and the Japanese army severely punished the escapees and their colleagues, so that eventually people no longer dared to escape and the guarding of the prisoners tightened up.

In April 1942, for the purpose of convenient management and security, the Japanese separated the officers and other ranks. Shamshuipo Barracks was used to imprison the other ranks, and all the officer class were moved to the concentration camp situated in Argyle Street. Also, because of the large number of Indian troops, all were sent to the Ma Tau Chung concentration camp, and eventually the Japanese army even released all the Indian troops for external propaganda. For reasons such as overcrowding, insufficient food, sanitary problems and shortage of medicines, epidemics of diseases broke out, infectious diseases such as dysentery, diphtheria and beriberi rampaged, especially in the extreme case of Shamshuipo Camp. Up to mid-1942 a total of over 300 prisoners of war in this camp died of sickness.

In August 1942, the operational territory of the Japanese army continued to expand. On the battlefield in China they had already penetrated northern China, central China and southern China, and in the south they had occupied places such as Hong Kong, Vietnam and Burma. The Japanese army had constructed fortresses and artillery pieces on various islands in the Pacific Ocean theatre, and traces of the Japanese army could be seen in places such as New Guinea, the Solomon Islands, Midway Island and the Ellice Islands,[23] as well as the Aleutian Islands and Attu Island.

In fact, such a small island nation did not have such huge manpower and material resources to deal with a theatre of war traversing half the Pacific Ocean. After mid-1942, the Japanese military campaign in the Pacific region started to suffer setbacks. All able-bodied men had already been sent to the battlefield. There was a severe shortage of labour resources, so the military government then started to make decisions about the prisoners of war imprisoned in various places.

In the Autumn of 1942, the Japanese army began transporting prisoners of war from various occupied areas back to Japan.

From Shamshuipo concentration camp in Hong Kong alone, about 3,000 prisoners of war were sent successively to places such as Osaka, Kobe and Nagasaki to become manual labourers, assisting the military government and domestic large scale industries in labouring work such as repairing roads, extending airports, mining and hauling.

War in the Pacific Ocean and Mainland China expanded continuously and military manpower resources were constantly being replenished, causing a drop in the labour force in Japan; therefore it was necessary to send the prisoners of war locked up in concentration camps back to Japan as a labour force.

Boarding the *Lisbon Maru*

On 25 September 1942, 1,816 [24] British prisoners of war assembled on the parade ground of Shamshuipo concentration camp. Lt Hideo Wada, interpreted by Niimori Genichiro, eloquently announced to the prisoners of war on the parade ground, "You will be taken away from Hong Kong to a beautiful country where you will be looked after and well treated. I shall lead this group. Please pay attention to your health and remember my face."

After the prisoners of war knew that they were to be sent to Japan, the effect on the morale of some of the men was extremely complex. Some still harboured illusions about Japan: they thought that Japanese people were concerned about "face", and should not be able to treat prisoners of war inhumanely in their own country, and so by being sent back to Japan they might be able to get better treatment. But other prisoners of war disagreed with what Lt Wada had said; they preferred to stay in Hong Kong, considering that this way they stood a better chance in the future of being rescued or escaping.

However, prisoners of war were of course unable to determine their own destiny. Following a simple physical examination, the prisoners of war were divided into groups of fifty, each group led by an officer, and they went by lighter from a jetty near Shamshuipo concentration camp to board a passenger-cargo vessel with a displacement of 7,152 tons – the *Lisbon Maru*. The *Lisbon Maru* had already been refitted: military equipment including small arms and communication equipment had been installed. The ship's captain was Kiyoda Shigeru; along with a crew of seventy-seven, all had been requisitioned by the Japanese military to be responsible for escorting the prisoners of war and other tasks.

According to international convention, ships carrying prisoners of war should fly the relevant flag or a clear sign to warn the enemy not to harm them. It is very clear that in this shipping operation the Japanese military had not done so, directly leading to the tragedy of the ship being sunk as a result of a surprise attack a few days later.

The *Lisbon Maru*. (NYK Museum)

The *Lisbon Maru.* (Combined Fleet)[25]

In fact, in the period from the outbreak of the Pacific Campaign to the end of the Second World War, Japanese merchant ships, crews and all, were constantly requisitioned by the Japanese Army and later sunk by allied forces. According to statistics, during the Second World War Japan lost altogether 2,394 merchant ships, which was eighty-eight percent of the total. And with respect to loss of life, speaking only of Japan's leading shipping company NYK, 5,300 sailors were lost this way.

The *Lisbon Maru* was just such a merchant ship flying the NYK flag requisitioned by the Japanese Army. After the ship had been sunk, the Japanese Army did not compensate the owner.

The representative of the prisoners of war was Lt Col HWM Stewart, Commanding Officer of 1st Battalion The Middlesex Regiment, assisted by a few other officers. Faced with nearly two thousand prisoners of war, the Japanese Army sent twenty-five guards commanded by Lt Hideo Wada to do guard duties. The British prisoners of war on board came from many fighting units, including officers and soldiers from 1st Battalion The Middlesex Regiment, 2nd Battalion The Royal Scots, the Royal Artillery, Royal Signals, Royal Engineers, Royal Navy, Royal Army Medical Corps and a few civilians.

British servicemen on board the *Lisbon Maru*[26]

No. 1 Hold	Royal Navy	379
No. 2 Hold	2nd Battalion, The Royal Scots	373
	1st Battalion, The Middlesex Regiment	366
	Royal Engineers	172
	Royal Corps of Signals	129
	Royal Army Medical Corps	22
	Royal Army Dental Corps	2
	Royal Army Service Corps	1
	Hong Kong Police Force	5
	Civilians	5
No. 3 Hold	Royal Artillery	360

Nearly two thousand prisoners of war were squeezed into three cargo holds: the Royal Navy, under the command of Lt JT Pollock, went into hold No 1 nearest the ship's bow; it was arranged for 2nd Battalion The Royal Scots, 1st Battalion The Middlesex Regiment, other minor units and unattached soldiers, commanded by Lt Col HWM Stewart, to go into hold number two, forward of the bridge; and the Royal Artillery, commanded by Maj Pitt, went into hold number three, abaft of the bridge. The holds were cramped. The air was hot and suffocating. Everyone had to sit crowded together shoulder to shoulder. They were pressed so tightly together that they could not lie down at the same time and rest and could only take it in turns to sleep.

Nearly one day after the prisoners of war had boarded the ship, on the afternoon of 26 September, about 778 Japanese soldiers, some of whom were wounded, boarded the *Lisbon Maru*, and took up most of the places on deck. These officers and soldiers had very excited expressions and they were talking and laughing, perhaps because they were going home to their country and their families. This made a strong contrast with the low spirits of the British prisoners of war in the holds below. At daybreak the following day the *Lisbon Maru* left the harbour and sailed north into the all-encompassing dangers of the open sea.

The Japanese army received intelligence informing them that US naval submarines were active in the seas along their route, and that they often made surprise attacks on Japanese commercial shipping en route so as to attack the Japanese military supply lines. Therefore, for security, the captain ordered the *Lisbon Maru* to sail as close to the shore as possible. Furthermore, the military frequently sent up reconnaissance aircraft from airfields along the coast to look for signs of submarines from high altitude. If one was found they could put in a large scale depth-charge attack.

On 30 September the weather was not bad. The *Lisbon Maru* had been sailing for four days, and on the whole everything was fine. However, so far as the prisoners of war locked up in the holds below were concerned, these few days were completely intolerable. The foul smell of sweat and faeces was suffocating. The Japanese army had to let some of the sick prisoners of war take turns on the deck to get some air.

However, according to the recollections of the prisoners of war, the diet they had at that time was OK. Breakfast was boiled rice and hot tea; and for the evening meal they also got a quarter of a tin of tinned beef and a tablespoon of vegetables. The food and water were also enough, and by chance they also got one or two cigarettes; but the toilet standards were seriously inadequate. Although during his trial after the War, the interpreter Niimori Genichiro insisted that every prisoner of war was issued with a life jacket, the surviving prisoners of war refuted this.

As far as the surviving prisoners of war were concerned, the experiences on the ship were unbearable to recall. According to the recollections of the prisoners, because the Japanese respected the Japanese emperor as a god, every morning they forced the prisoners to face towards Japan and make obeisance, which naturally everyone was extremely unwilling to do. But if anyone refused to co-operate they would get a blow from a Japanese army rifle butt and suffer maximum humiliation.

A US naval submarine attacks

During the Second World War both the Allies and the Axis powers had a policy of using submarines to attack enemy naval and civil shipping. The aim was to hope to hit the enemy's morale and deplete the enemy's supplies. Shipping that was attacked included warships, military transport ships, naval supply ships, military medical supply ships and even all merchant vessels commandeered for military use. In the faraway sea area of the Atlantic Ocean, Nazi Germany sent large numbers of U-Boats to intercept allied shipping crossing the ocean to obstruct the activities of US aid to Europe. And over here in the Pacific Campaign, US naval submarines adopted a similar strategy against Japan. They sent out submarine patrols in the East Pacific coastal area and successfully sank large numbers of passing Japanese commercial ships.

On the evening of 30 September, the USS *Grouper* SS 214, of the 81st Squadron of the US Pacific Fleet Submarine Force was carrying out its second sea patrol task in the waters of the Zhoushan archipelago. The submarine captain, LCDR Claren E Duke, and the other sailors had all come from Pearl Harbour Base lying more than 1,000 kms away.

That night the moon was bright, the sky was clear and the air fresh. It was good weather for distinguishing enemy and friendly shipping through the periscope. *Grouper* was submerged in the sea, quietly waiting for its prey. At about 4.00am in the early morning of 1 October the prey appeared. The *Grouper* discovered the tracks of the *Lisbon Maru* and some small sampans. LCDR Duke considered the moment opportune and decided to reduce the submarine's speed, lock onto the target and maintain a certain distance from it, and monitor the direction of the *Lisbon Maru*. The *Grouper* dived and advanced slowly at low speed for 4,000 yards, and after passing two fishing vessels it arrived at a predetermined area ahead of the *Lisbon Maru* and waited.

At that time, due to the limitations of submarine technology, submerged power was not good, and the general method of operations was to cruise on the surface and submerge only when going to battle stations after discovering a target. So submarines were normally equipped with guns for surface engagement and anti-aircraft use (like the *Grouper*'s 3-inch gun and .50-inch machine-gun and so on).

The US naval Gato class submarine USS *Grouper* SS214, which was cruising along the Western Pacific coastline at the time and carrying out the task of attacking commercial shipping.[27]
(Top: USN Photo # 5299-45 courtesy of Mare Island Museum.)
(Bottom: NH 90800 courtesy of US Naval History and Heritage Command).

On the morning of 1 October, after 6.00am, the sky was gradually brightening, the *Lisbon Maru* suddenly changed course and there was a chance it would diverge from the attack line determined by the *Grouper*. LCDR Duke immediately ordered the submarine to dive and immediately seized the opportunity to launch an attack. According to the *Grouper*'s logbook, at 7.04am the *Grouper* fired three torpedos at the *Lisbon Maru* at a range of 3,200 yards. Although this was not a long range, actually not one torpedo hit the target.

LDCR Duke gave the order again to fire the fourth torpedo, and after two minutes and ten seconds, the sound of a massive explosion came from the direction of the *Lisbon Maru*; the fuel tanks in the ship's belly had been hit by the submarine,[28] the ship immediately turned starboard fifty degrees and stopped. After assessing the battle situation through the periscope, LCDR Duke immediately ordered the submarine to change direction and sail to the starboard side of the *Lisbon Maru* and prepare to launch a new attack.

When the *Lisbon Maru* suddenly came under surprise attack from the US naval submarine, at first it flew a flag asking not to be damaged, and later the Japanese soldiers on the deck were firing in the direction of the submarine with their rifles. Even though this did not constitute a great threat to the submarine, at the least it demonstrated that the Japanese soldiers were reacting to the sudden attack.

At 8.45am the *Grouper*, lying on the West side of the *Lisbon Maru*, fired the fifth torpedo at a range of 1,000 yards. Five minutes later the torpedo passed close to the ship's hull and did not hit the target. The submarine crew again made new preparations, and at a depth of six feet prepared to launch the sixth torpedo. Just at this critical moment the *Lisbon Maru* listed slightly to starboard, just avoiding the attack path of this torpedo.

Thereupon the *Grouper* sailed to the port side of the *Lisbon Maru*, planning to attack from the ship's stern. At 9.37am the *Grouper* finally fired the sixth torpedo and scored a direct hit[29] on the *Lisbon Maru*. At this time a light bomber arrived in the airspace over the scene, forcing the *Grouper* to dive immediately to a depth of 100 feet, and whilst submerged they heard a tremendous sound. LCDR Duke probably never dreamed that he had ordered the sinking of a ship full of allied prisoners of war.

Tracks of the *Lisbon Maru* and the USS *Grouper*[30]

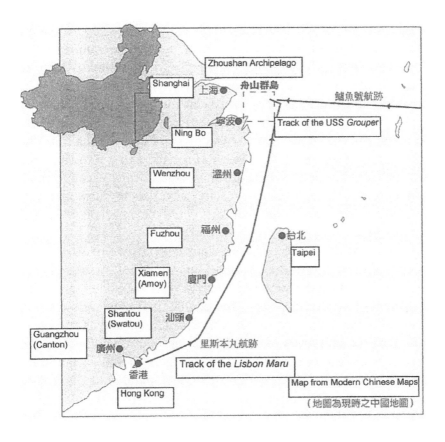

Mercilessly abandoned

The *Lisbon Maru* suffered a surprise attack as the sun was rising. A lot of prisoners of war had spent a night of torment: in the press and the stench it was difficult to get any sleep, and then they were awoken with a start and thought it was morning roll call time. They only heard the huge noise of the sounds of gunfire and felt the ship shaking and slowly come to a stop. The prisoners did not think they had been hit by a torpedo. From a small crack in the hatch cover they could see the Japanese soldiers on the deck were busily operating the ship's gun mounted on the bow of the *Lisbon Maru* and firing it towards the sea. In fact, it was only because the *Lisbon Maru* was an armed commercial ship and was not flying any flag to show she was carrying prisoners of war that she could be attacked by a US submarine.

According to the records, the Japanese army fired a total of ninety-eight rounds at the *Grouper*, but throughout was unable to repulse her. Originally there were a few wounded and sick prisoners of war on the deck, but at this time they were all sent back into the holds by the Japanese soldiers; and they posted guards at the entrances to strictly prevent any rebellion from the prisoners of war in the holds. The prisoners of war in the holds were not exactly clear about the developments taking place outside. Some of the representatives of the prisoners of war asked that some of them be allowed on deck to get some fresh air, but the Japanese army refused all the requests.

During the following hours, because the prisoners could not get out onto the deck, they could only guess wildly about the situation outside. They only knew that the normal food, water and lighting had been cut off. Men in the three holds thought of every possible way of exchanging information on the situation, including the use of Morse code, tapping on the pipes to pass on news. When they discovered that they were in the same dreadful situation, the prisoners could only hold out the fanciful hope that in the end the Japanese would rescue them.

The situation in number three hold amidships was the most wretched: water started coming in and the prisoners in the hold were forced to save themselves, taking turns in operating a hand pump to bale out the water. Many relatively robust prisoners used their utmost strength on the water pump, but many men passed out in the extremely hot, stuffy and airless atmosphere. But all this effort seemed to be to no avail: since there was a great deal of water coming in the ship's stern it was already gradually sinking; the hundreds of prisoners of war in hold number three were in imminent danger. At this time the Japanese military just sat there and did nothing. They did nothing to help.

In the afternoon the Japanese naval destroyer *Kuroshio* rushed to the waters near the *Lisbon Maru*. At about 5.00pm the 778 Japanese soldiers on board the *Lisbon Maru* started to transfer to the *Kuroshio*. Another Japanese cargo ship, the *Toyokuni Maru*, arrived on the scene at this time, and the commanders of all the warships assembled on the *Lisbon Maru* for a meeting. They concluded that the remaining Japanese troops should be transferred to the cargo ship, leaving a small guard and some sailors to watch the prisoners, and at the same time planned to tow the *Lisbon Maru* to shallow waters to await rescue.

To prevent disturbance from the nearly two thousand prisoners of war in the holds, the remaining twenty-five guards on the *Lisbon Maru* closed the hatches and kept them down with wooden battens. Col Stewart protested on behalf of the prisoners, requesting the Japanese army at least remove one of the battens to allow some air into the holds. Capt Kiyoda initially expressed some sympathy and quarrelled with Lt Wada over this. But finally Lt Wada insisted that he must close all the hatches and furthermore intimidated Capt Kiyoda: this was a military operation and he had no authority to interfere.

Thus, the holds for the prisoners of war were covered with tarpaulin tied down with strong rope, and the inside of the holds suddenly became pitch black. The prisoners of war provided each other with mutual support and comfort and with effort managed to remain calm and maintain discipline. There was no immediate trouble and they passed a very long night wide awake with fear.

At daybreak on 2 October, more than twenty-four hours after the *Lisbon Maru* had suffered a surprise torpedo attack, the ship began to sway violently from side to side, and it looked as if it was already impossible to reach shallow water before it sank. Lt Col Stewart decided to waste no more time and organised a small team to start operations. Lt Howell took the lead, and holding a knife, used every effort to cut upwards into a piece of wood and the tarpaulin covering the hatch. But through lack of air and his bodily strength not having the necessary stamina, the first effort did not succeed.

The *Lisbon Maru* sinking.[31]
National Archives UK (WO 235/1114)

At 8.10am, as the boat was about to sink, the captain sent a semaphore signal to the *Toyokuni Maru* asking permission to abandon ship. The cargo ship then sent lifeboats which took off most of the guards and sailors, leaving six or seven guards still on the deck keeping strict watch on the prisoners of war in the holds below.

By about 9.00am Lt Howell found another ladder leading up to the hatch cover, and using all his strength opened the hatch, and with Lt Potter of the Hong Kong St John Ambulance Brigade and four others climbed onto the deck and moved slowly towards the bridge, hoping to negotiate with the captain. However, the Japanese soldiers on the ship, without asking for any reason, suddenly began shooting at them. Lt Potter died on the spot.[32] Lt GC Hamilton was also wounded by rifle fire. The remaining two scurried into the hold. When Lt Col Stewart learned about the situation outside, he discovered that the side of the ship was already very low in the water, which meant there wasn't much time for them to escape with their lives.

At this time the last few Japanese guards and sailors left on the ship had been taken off. The towing ship had released the towline, leaving the *Lisbon Maru*, as well as the prisoners of war on the ship, to be buried together in the ocean.

The stern of the *Lisbon Maru* sank and a large volume of water rushed into hold number three, submerging the prisoners of war inside. At this time the prisoners of war in numbers one and two holds desperately rushed onto the deck and jumped into the sea to save their lives. Because most of the prisoners of war did not have life jackets, added to which half the men also were not equipped with life belts,[33] the majority desperately grabbed onto anything floating.

The Japanese army on the surrounding ships and boats saw this situation; and not only did they not lift a finger to rescue them, they even used machine-guns and rifles to kill the prisoners of war who had jumped into the water, or used their boats to run down the unfortunate prisoners. When on occasions a few prisoners of war with great difficulty climbed onto the cables hanging from the Japanese ships, they were savagely kicked off again by the Japanese soldiers. Many of the prisoners of war who originally would have been able to survive were thus killed in the sea by the Japanese army.

The Japanese naturally tried to cover up the real facts. A week after the incident took place, reports in the Korean and Japanese evening papers on 8 October said that a US submarine had sunk the *Lisbon Maru*, which was full of prisoners of war, and the Japanese army had made every effort to rescue them, but without success. They were trying to shirk their responsibility and put the blame on the allies. Naturally the report did not mention that the *Lisbon Maru* was not flying any prisoner-of-war ship flag, nor that when the cargo ship was sinking they had confined the prisoners of war to the holds and even shot and killed the prisoners of war who had escaped and jumped into the sea.

Rescue by fishermen

After the *Lisbon Maru* sank, the sea was full of scattered wreckage, corpses and rubbish. Hundreds of prisoners of war who were potential survivors were in the sea struggling for all they were worth. Because the Japanese army had not provided the ship with enough life buoys or lifeboats and similar equipment, those prisoners of war who were unable to grab hold of floating material who did not have the strength to carry on were swallowed up one after another by the merciless sea.

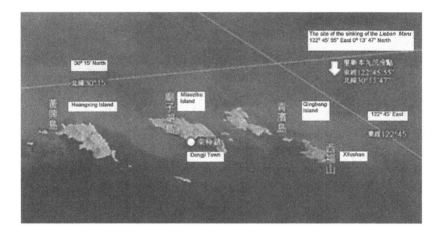

The site of the sinking of the *Lisbon Maru*. The residents of the nearby islands, who made their living by fishing, rescued the survivors on the basis of the fishermen's code, without considering whether they were Japanese soldiers or allied friends.[34]

The place where the incident happened was near the Zhongjieshan chain of islands at the extreme east of the Zhoushan archipelago, which includes the two small islands of Qingbang and Miaozihu. These were two totally isolated coastal islands with an area of about two square kilometres, and after the Japanese army occupied Zhoushan the two thousand fishermen on the islands were cut off from the outside world. At first, the fishermen actually did not know there had been a maritime disaster. They only saw cloth and other things scattered on the sea and were startled into discovering there had been a shipwreck only when the tide brought the prisoners of war towards the islands. Because the clothes of many of the prisoners of war were dilapidated, the fishermen could not distinguish whether they were Japanese or allied soldiers. But the fishermen believed that regardless of who they were, so long as they were floating on the sea, they had to rescue them. They threw into the sea the cloth and other things they had salvaged, and even the fresh fish, so as to make space to load even more victims. All the fishing households on Qingbang Island were mobilised by the five men – Zhao Xiaoru, Tang Pin'gen, Weng Azhou, Tang Ruliang and Xu Yusong – who told them it was a matter of life and death. They launched thirty fishing vessels, making forty-four rescue missions, saving 278 British prisoners, including the sixty-two saved by Xifushan Island.[35]

Miaozihu Island launched sixteen fishing boats, instigated by the five men, Shen Wanshou, Wu Qisheng, Lü Deren, Shen Yuanxing and Shen Aming, making twenty-one rescue missions, rescuing 106 British prisoners. Fishermen from both islands[36] spared no effort and continued the rescue until midnight, saving a total of 384 British prisoners.

Because the fishing boats had a limited capacity, they could only rescue around ten or so prisoners each time. Perhaps because they were exhausted, the prisoners did not jostle to be the first to squeeze onto the boats, but calmly waited for the next rescue by the fishermen. By going backwards and forwards again and again, the fishermen thus transported the prisoners, one small group at a time, back to the island. Many of the prisoners of war were unable to wait for the fishing boats to come back and pick them up, because they had used up nearly all their energy. They sank into the sea, never able to return home.

Because the wind was fast and the waves big, apart from those who drowned in the sea, some prisoners of war were unfortunately killed by being dashed onto the sharp rocks on the island by the waves. Arrangements were made for most of the British prisoners who were rescued and taken to Qingbang Island to stay temporarily in the Tian Hou Temple,[37] and the others stayed separately in the fishermen's homes. On Miaozihu Island all the British prisoners of war were taken care of in the individual homes of the villagers. Most of the British prisoners were wearing only shorts and vests; their clothing was extremely thin, and they had been through strenuous struggling in the sea. Their physical strength was spent, leaving them exhausted.

Despite the fishermen not having much food stored, seeing the wretched state of the prisoners of war, they generously gave all their rice, dried fish products, sweet potatoes and other food for the British prisoners to enjoy. At the same time, they each gave their coats to the British prisoners of war to wear. Because there was no common language, the fishermen did not know any details about the prisoners. They only knew that they should hand them over to the national government of the time as quickly as possible.

Veteran Dongji fisherman Shen Agui, with a sweet potato in his hand, gave a detailed account of the British prisoners being rescued that year and their hunger being allayed with sweet potatoes, rice and dried fish.

However, the effect of the sudden addition of more than 380 young men to these two small islands would create an immediate crisis in the supply of food. At the same time, several Japanese bombers flying over Qingbang dropped a large number of bombs in the area where the ship sank. The islanders were worried that the Japanese would come back again to round up the British prisoners, who were still in danger. Aware of this, Zhao Xiaoru, Tang Ruliang and others spent the whole night urgently discussing how to send the hundreds of prisoners of war to the interior and hand them over to the national government. They were frightened that, since the two islands were cut off from communication with the outside, in the event that they were discovered by the Japanese on the long and slow journey, the consequences would be disastrous. Up to daylight the following day, nobody had any sound strategy at all.

Captured again

On 3 October, five Japanese warships which had set off from the calm waters of Shenjiamen port reached Dongji waters. Three aimed the muzzles of their guns at Qingbang Island and two aimed at Miaozihu Island. After the ships pulled into the shore, Japanese army officers with swords in their hands, leading their soldiers, landed on the two islands and in an overbearing manner ordered the Japanese soldiers to do a house-to-house search, and one after another the British army officers and soldiers fell into enemy hands again.

According to the recollections related by the fishermen, the Japanese soldiers hung up and beat and tortured some of the fishermen and threatened to burn the village and kill everyone. The fishermen avoided adversity only when eventually an interpreter intervened, saying that saving people from maritime disasters was an ancient custom of fishermen. They had no intention of antagonising the Japanese. Some of the prisoners of war did not want to get the villagers into trouble and surrendered themselves to the Japanese soldiers. That afternoon the Japanese soldiers swaggered off escorting a total of 381 British prisoners from the two islands onto the warships.

The Japanese soldiers did not dream that in the face of their military force and intimidation the villagers had actually dared to conceal three of the prisoners of war. On Qingbang Island there is a sea cave called "Child Cave". Only one person can get through the entrance, but inside, the cave can hold around ten people. At high tide, the entrance to the cave is submerged by sea water, and seen from the outside, it is impossible to know of the cave's existence.

Early in the morning, when the Japanese warships pulled in, Tang Ruliang, Xu Yusong and others who were meeting at the time, immediately proposed to send the three British prisoners, AJW Evans, WC Johnstone and JC Fallace, to Child Cave behind Qingbang Mountain to hide. The young fisherman Weng Azhou volunteered to take these three men immediately into shelter and to assume responsibility for looking after their food and drink and their safety.

Child Cave which concealed three British prisoners of war.

For several days afterwards, Japanese warships repeatedly cruised in the area of the two islands, and left only on 8 October. So as to escort these three British prisoners to a safe zone, Zhao Xiaoru and more than ten others held further discussions and decided to send them quickly to the national government. The villagers sought the help of Miao Kaiyun, Second in Command of the Dinghai County 4th Regiment of the National Resistance Self Defence Corps, who lived in nearby Hulu Island. Miao Kaiyun had lived and studied in Shanghai when young and was rather good at English. Exchanges in the language of Evans and the others were smooth. He learned details of the maritime disaster, and immediately made careful arrangements to smuggle the British prisoners.

On the night of 9 October, the three British prisoners changed into fishermen's clothing and hid inside a small sampan rowed by the six men, Tang Pin'gen, Xu Atai, Li Chaohong, Guo Ade, Ren Xincang and Wang Xiangshui. Miao Kaiyun also sent an armed vessel to escort them, transferring the prisoners of war safely to the esteemed home of Miao Kaiyun's father-in-law, Yang Fu, on Hulu Island.

Evans and the other two received proper treatment in the Yang household: they changed into clean clothes and their morale rapidly stabilised. But after they had been there for day after day, they became restless, and all three became ill with fever to various degrees; Evans was the most serious. The Yang household, which had already made preparations for this, asked a doctor from Shenjiamen, Li Qiliang, to help diagnose and treat them. Following injections, medication and rest, and ten days of sweet potato rice porridge, at daybreak the three men's high temperatures abated. To get away from the danger zone as quickly as possible, Miao Kaiyun took some people to escort Evans and the others under cover of darkness. They took a boat to the Lu'an Regiment base in Guojugan and handed them over to Wang Jineng, Commander of the Dinghai County 4th Regiment of the National Resistance Self Defence Corps. In this way the three prisoners of war passed through many places with the assistance everywhere of the Resistance Self Defence Corps and reached the wartime capital, Chongqing, and were welcomed by the British Embassy in China.

The fate of the prisoners of war

Evans, Johnstone and Fallace faced hardships time and again. Finally they escaped from the evil clutches of the Japanese army and moreover they could live and expose to the world the

Japanese atrocity. They were interviewed by the press and radio and spoke of the *Lisbon Maru* tragedy, rebutting the claim of the Japanese side to have made every effort to save the prisoners of war.

However, the other prisoners who had been grabbed back by the Japanese army were not so lucky. On 5 October 1942 the captured prisoners assembled on the pier at Shanghai and once again carried out a morning roll call; the result was that there were only 970[38] remaining, which meant that almost half their compatriots had been entombed in the sea.

These unfortunate British Army prisoners of war included 235 men from the Royal Artillery, 160 from the Royal Scots, 150 from the Middlesex Regiment, 100 Royal Engineers, three from the Royal Army Medical Corps, three from the Naval Defence Unit[39] and two other men whose units are not known, totalling 635 men.

Prisoners of war sent to Moji Port in Kyushu. The prisoners of war were sent separately to Moji, Kobe and Osaka to perform hard labour, obtaining their release only after the Japanese surrender.

Apart from thirty-five suffering from relatively serious dysentery who stayed in Shanghai, more than 900 prisoners of war were escorted onto the merchant ship *Sensui Maru* and travelled a long way to prisoner-of-war concentration camps on the Japanese mainland. Five men died on the journey through rampant dysentery and diphtheria.

On 10 October 1942, the ship drew alongside at Moji and 36 people with serious diphtheria were sent to hospital. Of the remainder, a group of about 500 men were sent to Kobe and the rest were transported to Osaka.

Through a series of illnesses brought on by hard labour, the British prisoners were already extremely debilitated, and in the following months Lt Col Stewart and Lt Cuthbertson[40] died one after the other. During the first year in Japan, 114 men died in Kobe, fifty-five died in Osaka, twenty-one men died in Kokura, twenty-four men died in Moji and a further thirty men died in other places: 244 men altogether.[41]

Londoner Charles Heather, a *Lisbon Maru* survivor, was one of the first group of British Army Far East prisoners of war to return home.
(© Imperial War Museum (HU 93201))

In total, of the 1,816[42] men who boarded the *Lisbon Maru* at the beginning, 843[43] drowned or were murdered when the ship sank; five lost their lives en route to Japan, 244[44] men died one after another; altogether 1,092[45] men died and only 724[46] survived. These survivors returned to the UK and were reunited with their families after Japan was defeated.

The sea off the Zhoushan archipelago, Zhejiang Province

On 1 October 1942, the Japanese merchant ship the *Lisbon Maru*, carrying more than 1,800 soldiers from Hong Kong, was sunk by an allied submarine in this stretch of sea, and the generally forgotten story of people who made history began to unfold.

On the day the *Lisbon Maru* sank, fishermen made dozens of journeys in wooden fishing boats like the one in the picture, and brought prisoners of war who were floating in the sea and at their last gasp, one after another, to the shore.

"Regardless of whether they are westerners or orientals, once you see they are about to drown you must always go and rescue them." – A fisherman who took part in the rescue of prisoners of war from the sinking ship sixty years ago.

Dongji Town on Miaozihu Island today.
The fishermen who braved Japanese gunfire[47] at that time to rescue British soldiers
who were prisoners of war set off from this fishing port on Miaozihu Island.

Following detailed arrangements, in August 2008, former British Army gunner Charles Jordan,
one of the lucky survivors of the *Lisbon Maru* Incident,
returned to Dongji in the Zhoushan archipelago in Zhejiang Province and
met again the fishermen who had rescued more than 300 prisoners of war.

63

When Mr Jordan met the seven elderly fishermen who welcomed him, no-one could utter a word; they just hugged each other tightly, as if through their interlinked arms their profound feelings of friendship would become deeply embedded in each other. (*Zhoushan net*)

"Without them I would not be here today; my family would not be here today, my children... ."
– Charles Jordan

In the face of relentless searching by the Japanese army, fishermen found a place to hide some prisoners of war, a space in the rocks on the sea shore called, "Child Cave".

Charles Jordan, eighty-seven years of age, returning to Zhoushan, offering an English rose, the English national flower, to his comrades from the Incident in their eternal sleep in the ocean.

Digest

of

The *Lisbon Maru* Incident

Recollections of a Survivor of the *Lisbon Maru*

Zhoushan Daily: Written by Chen Yafang and Ni Ligang[48]

The weather on 18th August 2005 was fine and the temperature was between 25° and 32° C. At 8.30am a vessel belonging to the fishery administration set off from the fishing administration pier in Shenjiamen carrying some special guests and also carrying a solemn and touching story, and sailed to the most easterly occupied islands in the Zhoushan archipelago – Dongji.[49]

After we had been travelling for around two hours the outline of Miaozihu in Dongji could dimly be seen; the azure sea spread out like silk ahead of the boat, flocks of seagulls hovered, circling over the sea – this scene was so familiar that the events of sixty-three years previously slowly came back in the memory of a frail white-haired elderly foreigner.

Hong Kong under occupation: loss of freedom for the captured

Charles R Jordan was born in a small town near London in 1918. In his childhood and youth there was no way he could have anticipated that he would have a predestined sentimental bond with a small insignificant island in Chinese territory: the fishermen on this island gave him a second life.

After a long and arduous journey, the venerable eighty-seven-year-old, who already had difficulty walking, needed people to support his arms, but so as to be able to say "thank you" in person to the Dongji fishermen who had saved his life and those of his compatriots, he made light of travelling such a long way to reach the place that had appeared in his dreams countless times but that he did not want to remember. He did remember because of the kindness and courage of the Dongji fishermen, but wanted to forget because he could not bear to think of those of his compatriots who were victims buried at the bottom of the sea.

"In 1936 I enlisted in the army and became a gunner in the Royal Artillery. Then I was immediately posted to Burma. In 1937 I went with my unit to Hong Kong. In December 1941 the Japanese army launched an attack on Hong Kong. Even though we put up staunch resistance, in the end Hong Kong fell. I and other officers and soldiers such as Canadians and Australians[50] were captured by the Japanese and we lost our freedom."

Mr Jordan when he joined the army.

Because of his great age, the old man's memory of the war was beginning to fade. He could not remember in detail or clearly several of the situations at that time. But he made great efforts to remember, "I and other officers and soldiers were escorted on to the *Lisbon Maru* to go to Japan.

"The Japanese worshipped their emperor as a god. On the ship, every morning they forced us, including British, Canadians and Australians[51] to face the direction of the emperor and kowtow. But we were extremely unwilling to do this and just went through the motions, so we were often fiercely beaten by the Japanese. But we took it and didn't shed any tears." Finding it unbearable to remember the days on the ship, the old man was unwilling to recall any more.

No understanding of currents: fortunately rescued

In the small hours of 1 October 1942, when the *Lisbon Maru* was hit by a torpedo fired from the American naval submarine USS *Grouper* and sank, twenty-four-year-old Mr Jordan had no understanding of currents, but relying on the instinct of self-preservation and will-power, he and other compatriots rushed out of the hold and leapt into the sea, fleeing for their lives.

On 8 August 2005, Charles Jordan, at the venerable age of eighty-seven, once again returned from England to the Zhoushan Archipelago in Zhejiang Province and met the fishermen who had saved his life sixty years previously.

"I couldn't swim, and with another compatriot I clung tightly to a piece of wood floating on the sea and followed the movement of the waves. I don't know how long for, but I was already exhausted. Eventually fishermen rowing a sampan saved me and took me ashore. Although my memories of how I fled for my life are very vague, there is one thing I remember clearly: in the fisherman's home, the honest and friendly fisherman cooked sweet potatoes for me and made green tea, which restored my strength.

"This was the first time I felt free since being captured. Without the help of the fishermen I basically would not have been able to escape the evil hands of the Japanese army, so I wholeheartedly thank those courageous fishermen, who risked being punished by the Japanese army to save us."

The old man probably did not know that actually the magnanimous act of the Zhoushan fishermen saved even more lives, because they prevented a possible hidden crime. British army prisoner of war survivor 2Lt Geoffrey Hamilton said in his reminiscences, "The original idea of the Japanese was to let all the prisoners of war drown; that way they could say the ship had been sunk by the Americans and they had had no opportunity to carry out a rescue. Later, once the Japanese army saw that the Chinese had rescued so many prisoners of war, they realised they could not carry out their plan and changed their policy."

Return to the UK: Friends become a family

In addition to his elder son Alan R Jordan and his younger son Richard S Jordan, his inseparable eighty-five-year-old wife Evelyn D Jordan also accompanied Mr Jordan on this visit to Zhoushan as one of the survivors of the *Lisbon Maru.*

"Our relationship began before the Second World War: we became pen-friends through writing letters, but we had never met. Then I joined up and left the UK. We met for the first time in 1942[52] when I returned to the UK; I was then twenty-four. We married in 1946. Next year is our 60th wedding anniversary, our diamond wedding." The elderly lady spoke of her romance with her husband and their happy marriage with a sweet smile.

After they were married, Mr and Mrs Jordan brought up five children, three daughters and two sons, and now have ten grandchildren and one great grandson: it's a fine harmonious family.

At the banquet held on the evening of 17 August 2006[53] to welcome the British army survivor of the *Lisbon Maru* disaster and his family visiting Zhoushan, Mr Jordan presented the Municipal Party Committee and the Municipal Government with a set of photographs which recorded his life: his innocent appearance as a child; his bearing in uniform when he joined the army, and a picture of a happy family....

At a press conference in Dongji Town, the old soldier and the elderly fishermen
recount stories of that time. The *Lisbon Maru* incident aroused interest
in a lot of the mainland media, and local Party and Government bodies
and others are taking seriously reshaping their work on this historic incident.

He said sincerely, "Without the kindness and courage of the Dongji fishermen, I would not have lived to return to the UK and start a family, and this large family of mine would not exist today, nor would you be able to look at these photographs."

The dusty past: the family finally understand

When a reporter asked the old man's younger son Richard whether when he was young his father had often spoken about his alarmingly dangerous experiences, the surprising answer was this. "When I was young, my father never spoke about his experiences in the army nor of being in distress and getting rescued. He told me his story only ten years ago, when I was thirty-five. That was the first time I heard about it so I was utterly astounded: the cruelty of the Japanese army and the kindness of the Dongji people left me deeply shocked."

The elderly Mrs Jordan said to reporters, "After Charles and I were married, he never told me the moving story of the misfortune he suffered and being rescued by Dongji fishermen. I learned about it only after he joined a retired soldiers association and I saw an article he had written about the *Lisbon Maru*."

Face up to history: Japan should apologise

"Japan's treatment of all occupied nations was exceptionally inhumane. I think that, when the *Lisbon Maru* sank, the Japanese army should have rescued us. But they didn't care if you were British, Canadian or Australian;[54] they stood by and looked on at all of us unconcerned, allowing us to die. This was cruelty in the extreme. And yet the Japanese have always believed that the war they conducted was right. They have never acknowledged their history of aggression," said Mr Jordan.

During the old man's unhurried and halting recollections, the boat slowly drew alongside Miaozihu pier. Here, his sleeping memories were awakened; in August in Dongji, the place which had given him a second life.

For several decades Mr Jordan never mentioned to anyone – including to his wife and children – his experiences in the *Lisbon Maru* incident which were unbearable to recall.

Charles Jordan and his elder son Alan Jordan giving a speech
at the banquet welcoming Mr Jordan.

The Jordan family – the elder son Alan and younger son Richard – accompanied
their parents on their visit to far-away China to relive history. When the war was over,
Mr Jordan returned home and married, raising five children. As well as the two sons
who accompanied their elderly father to China, Mr Jordan also has three daughters.

BUCKINGHAM PALACE

The Queen and I bid you a very warm welcome home.

Through all the great trials and sufferings which you have undergone at the hands of the Japanese, you and your comrades have been constantly in our thoughts. We know from the accounts we have already received how heavy those sufferings have been.   We know also that these have been endured by you with the highest courage.

We mourn with you the deaths of so many of your gallant comrades.

With all our hearts, we hope that your return from captivity will bring you and your families a full measure of happiness, which you may long enjoy together.

George R.I.

September 1945.

A letter signed by King George V[55] of England
after the end of the Second World War
to prisoners of war returning home.

HEADQUARTERS EIGHTH ARMY
UNITED STATES ARMY
OFFICE OF THE COMMANDING GENERAL

20 September 1945

To Gnr. Jordan, Charles Rivers, RA:

As commander of the United States Eighth Army, it is my privilege to extend to you the heartfelt thanks of your American allies for the splendid spirit of generosity and unselfishness you have displayed these past two weeks.

In volunteering to remain in your prison camp to assist in the liberation of your comrades, you have proved again that the strength of the United Nations is built on that most solid of foundations - fellowship of man.

We of the Eighth Army are proud to be your liberators. We congratulate you on your newly gained freedom and wish for you the best of good luck, good health and happiness in the years to come.

Most sincerely yours,

R. L. EICHELBERGER
Lieutenant General, USA
Commanding

A personal letter sent to British Army prisoner of war Jordan from the Headquarters of the United States Eighth Army.[56]

Let the sunken *Lisbon Maru* be a testimony to friendship
Zhoushan Net report[57]

Sixty-three years ago, the *Lisbon Maru*, carrying 1,816[58] British prisoners of war, sank in the waters of Dongji, Zhoushan. The simple, kind-hearted Zhoushan fishermen spontaneously took out their fishing boats, risking death to rescue them from the sea, giving the peoples of the two nations undying friendship. Sixty three years later Mr Jordan, one of the survivors, and his family, full of feelings of gratitude, came thousands of miles from far way across the oceans to China, to Zhoushan, to Dongji, just so that he could say "Thank you" in person to the elderly fishermen who had taken part in that rescue.

At the venerable age of eight-six, Mr Jordan is grey-haired. He said to reporters, "For more than sixty years I have always dreamed of these simple, kind-hearted life-saving benefactors, hoping that I could return to Zhoushan whilst still alive, but I've never been able to." This really was a rare opportunity. When the telegram from Zhoushan looking for survivors reached him, he could not control his feelings of gratitude. At last this was it: this would answer his lifetime's wish.

A man of advanced years: gratitude from afar

At 8.00am the elderly Mr Jordan boarded the fishery administration vessel with an excited face as he would finally be able to see his benefactors from whom he had been separated for more than sixty years. As soon as the boat moved off, the old man started frequently looking out of the window. And later, as Dongji got nearer and nearer, he seemed more and more restless. When I told him that the fishermen who had taken part in the rescue that year had come to the pier in person to greet him, the old man's expression became excited.

At 10.20am the fishery authority boat, fully laden with undying friendship between the peoples of two nations, unhurriedly drew into the side of Dongji pier. With his arms supported by those accompanying him, old Mr Jordan hurried out of the cabin. A welcoming throng stood filling both sides of the pier. The island children were holding national flags and calling out, "Welcome, welcome; warmly welcome!" On seeing such a warm picture, the old man immediately smiled. Without considering his fatigue from the journey, he went forward and embraced the children, just as though all those he saw were his own relatives. When Mr Jordan and the seven elderly welcoming fishermen met, everyone was unable to speak, they just embraced tightly. It seemed as if that profound friendship wanted to embed itself deeply inside the other through their interlinking arms.

Facing each other: common memories of that year

At 1.10 in the afternoon, the Jordan party and representatives of the elderly fishermen who had taken part in the rescue at the time sat down for a chat. Old Mr Jordan sat opposite the elderly fishermen Chen Yonghua and Shen Agui and others. They looked at each other and spoke excitedly about the situation of the sinking of the *Lisbon Maru*.

More than 190 fishermen used their small sampans to rescue over 300 British Army prisoners of war in the ever-changing Zhoushan open seas. Today, more than sixty years later, many fishermen and prisoner of war survivors are no longer with us.

Mr Jordan said, "At the time we were floating on the ice-cold sea. There were large stormy waves and I was a non-swimmer. A comrade and I clung onto a plank of wood floating on the sea and we thus floated and drifted with the tide. We were rapidly losing consciousness and had absolutely no idea where we were going. Eventually the island fishermen rescued us. They gave us the only food they had – sweet potatoes – and gave us clothes to wear. I am really grateful to them: without them I would not be here today, this family would not be here today, my children..." His voice faded.

Old Chen Yonghua gesticulated with both hands as he spoke about the scene that year of picking people up to save them, "At that time it was just daylight. We fisherman were already up. Suddenly we heard a huge sound from the sea, "Bang!" and we all ran out to look. A large steamship was sinking. At first it was the stern that sank, and after an hour the bow had also sunk. At this time there were lots of goods and cloth and so on from the ship floating on the sea. We all rowed out our sampans to fish things out of the sea. As we neared the goods we discovered – my goodness – there were also lots of people floating. Of course, saving people was important, so we saved them. A vast area of sea was full of men's heads. We launched all our sampans, making trip after trip to save people!"

The seven elderly fishermen who that year had courageously rescued British prisoners of war vied to speak. Their faces were quite unaffected. Their guileless answers were ordinary and natural:

"Nothing is more important than human life!"

"So long as people were still alive, how could we watch them die?"

"Regardless of whether they were westerners or orientals, so long as we could see them about to sink, we had to go and save them."

The elderly Charles looked intently at the benefactors in front of him who had saved lives. "At that time they themselves were also basically suffering from hunger, yet they gave us food and accommodation..."

Old Lin Fuyun gave a broad generous smile, "It's all very well rescuing them; could we then let them freeze to death or starve to death? That's a characteristic of us fishermen."

A vast expanse of billowing waves: mourning the souls of the dead

At 2.00pm everyone took the fishery authority boat to the area where the *Lisbon Maru* incident had happened, to mourn the souls of the dead. The elderly Mr Jordan stood in the bow of the boat, facing the blue water of Qingshan ahead of him with a solemn and respectful expression, as if remembering that tragic and moving scene of sixty-three years previously.

At this time Mr Jordan was silent. He clutched a rose and gazed steadfastly at the water. He seemed to be talking about something. Probably he was quietly praying for his silent comrades here, giving their souls a sense of home, so they would not be troubled by home-sickness. The people accompanying him also cast fresh flowers into the sea one after another.

An elderly fisherman gives a detailed account to the press covering Mr Jordan's visit to Dongji of his feelings on being reunited.

81

Fresh flowers were thrown into the ocean one after another carrying deep feelings of grief and cherished memories, each fresh flower representing one soul, each sustaining a cherished memory. Bobbing up and down in the ripples of the blue ocean, they were gradually carried further away by the ocean waves. The salty wet sea breeze could not blow away the grief and heartbreak of past events. The leisurely sea could not carry away the undying friendship between the peoples of the two nations. The sunken *Lisbon Maru* witnessed everything.

Oral Account of History:
"Father did what Chinese people should do"
Oral recollection: Miao Zhifen,
written record collated by Wang Yongjian[59]

I am the only daughter of Mr Miao Kaiyun. I feel extremely proud that in that historic incident father did what Chinese people should do.

When a lot of survivors were rescued by the Qingbang fishermen and taken to the island, Qingbang Island fisherman Tang Ruliang discovered that three of them were different to the mass of the barefoot survivors: they were supported by the arms by the other barefoot survivors when they came ashore. Tang Ruliang knew through explanations in not very fluent Hong Kong Cantonese by some of the foreign survivors who had lived for many years in Hong Kong, that amongst the victims of the disaster these three barefoot survivors were leaders with special status. Tang Ruliang immediately prepared to take these three to stay in his own home.

Early the next day (3 October), Tang Ruliang sent his young brother-in-law Wang Bangrong first to go and ask his good friend Weng Achuan, whose home was in Nantian Bay, to make arrangements to prepare a hiding place for three survivors with special status. As Nantian Bay was quite a long way from Nan'ao and also relatively remote, it was an inconspicuous and peaceful little village. In the afternoon, as the sun was setting in the west, Tang Ruliang personally escorted the three foreigners with special status to Weng Achuan's home. Weng Achuan let the three foreigners hide in Child Cave during daylight and in the evening took them back home to spend the night.

Early on the third day (4 October), the foreigners who had been rescued discovered that the three leaders living in Tang Ruliang's home had disappeared. Then the foreigners, who did not understand the real situation, gathered in the room in the Tian Hou Temple in Qingbang Island and gesticulated at Qingbang Island's VIP Tang Ruliang (Note: because they were afraid that their own three leaders had had an accident).[60] Only through patient explanation by Ruliang and the others did they mollify the misunderstandings and suspicions of the foreigners. After dinner,

Tang Ruliang reckoned they should avoid any misunderstanding, so on the quiet he selected some foreigners' representatives and took them to Weng Azhou's home in Nantian Bay and surreptitiously called on and paid respects to the three foreigners with special status. Moreover they took orders from the three leaders to all the survivors, then everyone understood that the Chinese Qingbang Island fishermen were doing what they could to contact the anti-Japanese resistance guerrilla forces outside, to enable the whole body of survivors to get to the mainland and return to their countries. Living separately was a means to safeguard them.

Just as the villagers' General Secretary Zhao Xiaoru and Chairman of the villagers' representative Committee Tang Pin'gen with Tang Ruliang, Xu Yusong, Li Chaohong, Ren Xincang, Wang Xiangshui, Weng Azhou and others were discussing sending an officer to contact the Dingxiang guerrilla command post Resistance Self Defence Regiment (The 4th Regiment) to rescue the foreign allied soldiers, five Japanese naval warships had surrounded all the islands of Dongji. Furthermore, in the afternoon they began a targeted clean-up from many different directions of the two islands of Qingbang and Miaozihu. Perhaps in order to protect the three with special status and so as not to add to the troubles of the ordinary people on the islands, when the foreigners living in the temple and the fishermen's homes heard the sound of their comrades blowing whistles, they came out and assembled of their own accord and were immediately escorted onto a warship by the Japanese soldiers. Only the three with special status who had been hidden by the fishermen in Little Bay Cave [61] in Nantian Bay on Qingbang Island had a lucky escape from being captured.

Tang Ruliang's wife Wang Jiaoyun and Weng Azhou's wife Liu Anü as well as her daughter Weng Liuxiang[62] took food and water every day to the three foreigners hiding in Child Cave, but they were extremely worried about what to do if the Japanese army should ever find out. The situation was extremely dangerous at that time because every day Japanese gunboats were patrolling between every island, large and small, in the Zhoushan archipelago and checking everything thoroughly.[63]

After urgent discussions between Tang Ruliang and his elder brother Tang Pin'gen, they immediately reported the situation on Qingbang Island, through Zhao Xiaoru, to the Deputy Head of Dongji Township, Shen Pinsheng, who lived on Miaozihu Island. They knew that Shen Pinsheng had good connections with my father's 4th Regiment of the anti-Japanese Resistance. So Shen Pinsheng right away sailed with Wu Qisheng (Head of the old people's home) of Miaozihu Island to find Regimental Second-in-Command Miao Kaiyun,[64] who was currently staying with Hu Ludao's father in law, to ask for his help. After my father had heard the urgent report from Shen Pinsheng and Wu Qisheng, he immediately led his personal bodyguard and four or five other guards, with Shen Pinsheng and Wu Qisheng leading the way, risking interrogation by Japanese patrol boats, to hurry to Little Bay Cave[65] on Qingbang Island that same night to pay a call on the three foreigners. Because my grandparents had worked for many years in Shanghai for a telephone company run by a foreigner, my father was born in Shanghai and completed primary school and junior middle school in Shanghai. He then went to work for a commercial printer in Shanghai and taught himself several foreign languages.

Mr Miao Kaiyun, who took part in the rescue of British Army prisoners of war in the Zhoushan archipelago, is the father of the author of this article.

It was only after exchanges between my father and the three foreigners that they knew the three foreigners were British allied soldiers in the War of Resistance[66] against Japan, one of whom was an Englishman named Evans who was sick and running a fever, but very talkative (at that time he was the Chief Inspector of the Hong Kong tobacco factory of British American Tobacco).

The other two, called Johnstone and Fallace, were a senior official on the staff of the British Governor of Hong Kong and a Royal Navy Sub Lieutenant in the Indian Fleet. These two did not talk very much.[67] My father felt this was a very important matter and they should quickly try to send these three British allies to the mainland as soon as possible.

To this end, my father made a quick decision and instructed Shen Pinsheng and the others to make careful arrangements and security measures for this. At the same time he sent Lu Ruiyuan with a guard to go quickly to the Shens' home to report to his father-in-law old Mr Yang Fulin,[68] and to ask him for some money to get a doctor to Hulu Island. Afterwards, that night, my father took a boat back to Guoju, the location of the 4th Regiment, and separately sent people to report to Wang Jineng, head of the garrison areas Liuheng, Taohua, Shijiajian and Putuoshan in Dinghai County, and concurrently Commander of the 4th Regiment of the Ding-Xiang anti-Japanese resistance guerrillas, who was at Kangtou consolidating and training troops, and also to report to Su Benxi, Head of Dinghai and Xiangshan Counties.

After Lu Ruiyuan and the others had reached the Shens' home and found my maternal grandfather (Yang Fulin), they lost no time in reporting the situation to old Mr Yang, who immediately wrote a letter to give to the visitors and exhorted them again and again, "You must really, really watch out for your security, and make absolutely sure you are not seen by the Japanese. Take this letter to Hulu Island and give it to my wife. She will be able to co-ordinate matters for you, and I will immediately get a doctor to go there. This business must succeed without fail." When Lu Ruiyuan and the others got back to make their report to the Guoju troops, it was already the second half of the night; my father convened another urgent meeting with the help of old Mr Yang, and carefully arranged the detailed plan for the transfer and escort of the three British allies.

It was another calm and tranquil night. Three fishermen, brothers-in-law Yuan Rukang (nicknamed little pickerel and puffer fish – married), Guo Ade (eighteen years old at the time) and Guo Dakang, from Qingbang Island in Dongji County, under careful arrangements made by their father-in-law Tang Pin'gen, fifth uncle Tang Ruliang and other relatives and friends, in

86

accordance with my father's operational route, using a small sampan, put make-up on the three British allies, carefully disguised them dressed in old fishermen's clothes, simple tops and loose black fishermen's trousers, and hid them under the roof of the sampan. After reloading the fishing baskets, the three brothers-in-law rowed to Hulu Island. My father also sent a pair of escort boats and personally supervised the formation, following closely to prepare against interception by Japanese patrol boats. That night the wind and tides were favourable and the journey went smoothly. The small boat travelled for over three hours, and finally they safely reached Hulu Island beach (that is Aomenkou on Hulu Island).[69] Guo Ade and the other brothers-in-law handed over the sick and feverish Evans, and Johnstone and Fallace who were supporting him by the arms, to Yu Dengnian and others from reinforcements of the 4th Regiment on Hulu Island who were waiting for them. Soon after the three brothers-in-law had left in their boat, my father's escort boats reached Hulu Island. Moving quickly in the dark (they were afraid to light a lamp) they supported the three British allies and took them to the courtyard of the Yangs' house. My grandmother immediately called people to "Close the gate, we don't want news of this to spread". My aunt, Shi Lanxian (who was about twenty-seven at the time), was very kind-hearted and understanding and immediately changed the soaking wet clothes of the three British men for dry ones.

That night all three of the British men had different stages of fever. After not a very long time my grandfather hired a fishing boat from Shenjiamen and went to Hulu Island and spent a huge sum of money to get a doctor called (probably) Li Qiliang (at that time he was a medical MSc). After injections, taking medicine and rest, by daylight their fever had abated, and they ate hot steaming sweet potatoes and porridge.

Evans was even more voluble, "Oh; OK! I've never eaten such delicious food before. The Japanese robber bandits put my whole family on the ship, and after the *Lisbon Maru* accident, I saw with my own eyes my wife and son being taken away by the waves, and I had no way of rescuing them.[70] "I myself didn't want to live, but it was you kind-hearted Chinese people that risked death to save me and my comrades. If we can get back to our homes, we will definitely repay you Chinese people's great kindness. We won't break our word!"

Miao Zhifen, the only daughter of Mr Miao Kaiyun of the 4th Regiment of the Dinghai County National Resistance Self Defence Regiment. Mr Miao Kaiyun spent his early years growing up in Shanghai, understood some English and could communicate with the British prisoners of war.[71]

It was only then that my grandfather and father clearly understood their own position. My father there and then said, "Sir, you are wrong. We don't save people so as to have kindness repaid. Furthermore we have money. We are concerned only that you will be able to return safely to your country!" After daybreak, Dr Li left some medicine and followed my grandfather back to the Shen house. In the morning, Weng Xianfang, a prominent figure on Hulu Island, heard that in the middle of the previous night lots of people had gone to old Mr Yang's house and now the gate was shut tight. He hurried over to Yang's house and knocked on the gate.

At this time my father heard old Mr Weng knocking on the gate and hurriedly hid the three British allies behind the main room, then ceremoniously opened the gate and welcomed old Mr Weng. When Mr Weng entered the gate, he asked, "Son-in-law (my father was Yang's son-in-law), uncle is not being very polite today, what secret are you hiding from me?" My father knew old Weng was a senior member of the old generation and told him about saving the people. When old Weng heard this he said very anxiously, "Son-in-law, I beg you, our Hulu Island is small, everyone lives in thatched cottages; once the East Ocean people (i.e. the Japanese)[72] know about this, they could burn Hulu Island to the ground. You don't want to hurt me and everyone, I must order you to send them away.

At that my father said to old Weng, "Please relax, old Weng. I shall send them away as soon as it's dark. But please will old Weng of the older generation guarantee to keep this a secret. Tell others that the Yang house has been making arrangements for his birthday celebrations." Thus, through injections from an outstanding doctor, taking medicine and rest, the three British allied soldiers made a speedy recovery. Evans and my father exchanged gifts. The three of them also wanted to take my father's photograph and mementos as souvenirs. But it is a pity about the souvenir given to my father by the British men because, on 14 June 1947, the commander of The Third Company of the National Dinghai County security police Wang Xueyu, the director of the Shenjiamen police military joint defence office and others, suspicious of contacts between my father and communist party member Xu Xiaoyu, killed him and then searched and looted the house.

That night, escorted by special boats belonging to Dongji Township Vice Mayor Shen Pinsheng and others, my father took the three British allies straight to Ganlu Convent[73] in Guoju,[74] where the 4th Regiment of the Ding (hai) Xiang (shan) Anti-Japanese Resistance Self-Defence Regiment was stationed. At that time the Regimental Commander Wang Jineng got the report from my father. He immediately went to the troops' base and after visiting the three British allies he immediately said to my father, "Younger brother, you and I can be proud and elated today!" My father replied, "Elder brother, what you say is in very poor taste. You can say that only to me, absolutely not to anyone else outside. You and I must maintain the dignity and national prestige of the Chinese people". Wang replied, "Everyone calls us sworn brothers, what can we two brothers not say to each other? Since we've rescued people, let's take a photograph as a memento and to leave evidence of the rescue."

Centre is grandmother Weng Liuxiang who took food to the British soldiers at the time. On the left is Mr Kent Shum, Secretary of the Hong Kong *Lisbon Maru* Association, who went all the way to Zhoushan to visit the elderly fishermen. The two people at the back are reporters from the mainland press.

The three British guests also eagerly asked to be photographed with my father and Wang Jineng, as well as with those who had come to see them off: the Vice Mayor of Dongji Township Shen Pinsheng; Wu Qisheng, Head of the old people's home; security guard platoon commander Dou Feiyun (Xiong); Xin Yuanyin and others. After the photographs, Wang spoke to my father again:

"Younger brother, this sending off of the three British guests will need agreement from higher up, and will also need a lot of money. Although I have a large family, you know that economically we cannot make ends meet." My father promptly replied, "Elder brother, please put your mind at rest. I can arrange all of this, you just relax and go back to the training unit, and that will be fine." The next day Wang Jineng, having mutually embraced and bid farewell to the three British allies, returned to the training unit.

Through many careful arrangements, my father finally sent Xin Yuanyin (now eighty-seven years old, in 1998 he wrote "Record of Personal Experiences Escorting and Rescuing British Military Prisoners of War" and similar reminiscent articles),[75] Chen Genyou, Jiang Mingyuan and sixteen others (NB: and gave a lot of travel expenses) to escort the three British men to Xiangshan. Then men sent by Su Benxi, head of the national government Ding (hai) and Xiang (shan) counties, escorted them to the Zhejiang provincial government (War of Resistance) base in Yunhe County and they were then transferred to the British consulate in China in the capital Chongqing. The exposure on Chongqing radio by the three British men of the inhumane actions of the Japanese army caused international public anger and condemnation, thus enabling the other 381 *Lisbon Maru* survivors to get back alive to the British Isles[76] and be reunited with their families after the Japanese unconditional surrender.

It is now more than sixty years since the events of the rescue of the British soldiers. What my father did was just what any Chinese should do. Now the appropriate bodies are making films and other works of art to recall these deeply ingrained memories of past events, and the Municipal Communist Party Committee Propaganda Department has also taken the lead in officially setting up the Historical Research Association and has achieved encouraging progress, with the sustained efforts of the Municipal Committee, the City Government and people of insight from all fields, taking this opportunity through recollections and specially drafted articles to commemorate this cherished moving moment of history and for public reference.

Due to the passage of time, much valuable primary source material has been lost, and unavoidably there will be some incomplete places. I hope that people of insight in the community will continue to work together to enable this historical moment to reappear authentically and that this will play the role it should in developing the burgeoning of Zhoushan's economy and culture.

Finally, I should like to thank everyone for the painstaking efforts they have made in enabling this earth-shaking piece of history during the Second World War to see the light of day again! Thanks to all those who were still able to remember after so many years my staunch, kind-hearted and respected father! Thanks to all leaders and comrades!

Tales of *Lisbon Maru* memorabilia
From *Zhejiang Online*[77]

A mouth organ, it is said, has gone to Shanghai. An elderly fisherman told me that, at the time, Qingbang fisherman Zhang Fuqing's boat went to sea to rescue people. The boat was already full of British prisoners of war, but Zhang Fuqing heard the sound of music coming from a reef to one side and rowed the boat to the side of the reef. There were three British prisoners of war on the reef, one of whom was playing a mouth organ. The intention was clear: they hoped someone would be able to save them. Eventually, the British prisoner of war who was playing the mouth organ went into the sea, hung onto the side of Zhang Fuqing's boat and swam to Qingbang Island.

To thank him for his kindness in rescuing him, the British prisoner gave the mouth organ to Zhang Fuqing. Therefore many Qingbang Island fishermen knew that the Zhang family had a special mouth organ. But not long afterwards, because life was really hard, Zhang Fuqing's wife took the mouth organ to Shanghai and exchanged it for a hectolitre of grain.

Liu Zhuding who is forty-four years old this year lives in Lujiazhi in Shenjiamen in Putuo District. His grandparents took part in the rescue of British prisoners of war in Qingbang at that time, but both have passed away. Because of a typhoon, I could not cross to Lujiazhi on the coast opposite Shenjiamen and could only make contact by telephone. Liu Zhuding said to me on the telephone, "When my grandmother died she gave me this ring. It is engraved with JNW 9.375." According to what Liu Zhuding said, the ring was presented as a memento by one of the rescued British prisoners of war, and his grandmother urged him again and again that if there was ever an opportunity in the future he should give it back to British friends.

Early on the 23rd day of the eighth month in the lunar calendar in 1942 Liu Zhuding's maternal grandmother went down to the shore, set sail and started fishing. Suddenly there was a huge "boom" sound from the surface of the sea. Those at home did not know what had happened. They were shocked, and waited. Soon they saw a large ship trailing thick smoke sailing slowly in the direction of Qingbang Island. My grandfather, paternal grandmother and uncle all watched from the shore and saw the large ship suddenly sink. At first there were lots of people floating on the water, like ants. And soon afterwards they saw cloth and other goods also floating on the water.

After those people had been rescued, grandmother saw that their clothes did not cover their bodies. She got some clothes from home and gave them to them to wear, and also gave them some towels to dry themselves. In the end, three people were helped to escape by concerned locals. Before they departed, one of them took the ring off his finger and put it in Liu Zhuding's hand, and with tears flowing made a long speech. My grandmother did not understand, but looking at their gestures, it seemed as if he was saying, "Please keep this ring safe. In the future it will be a symbol of our relationship."

The background history of this small ring
has been buried for several decades.[78]

Searching for the *Lisbon Maru*
Reflections on visiting Dongji[79]

(1) **Sherwin Chan**

Since February 2005, I have been in contact with Mr Jordan's family and the Donald sisters[80] by telephone and E-mail. The first impression I had was that they were very approachable. I was just an ordinary student in the UK making contact with them, but from start to finish they showed a trusting attitude towards me, which made me very happy, linking up with strange foreigners whom I had not previously had the pleasure of meeting. They were eagerly looking forward to coming thousands of miles to faraway China, which they already knew to be a strange country. One has to admire their courage.

Looking back on it now, the profound significance to the Jordan family and the Donald sisters of this journey to China was certain to be far reaching. Think about it: the *Lisbon Maru* incident took place more than sixty years previously in the sea opposite Dongji. Mr Jordan would not have escaped with his life had he not been rescued by the fishermen there. And they went to the area of the shipwreck lying forever in Chinese waters, sorrowfully following the uncles of the two Donald sisters, so I thought that visiting the site again[81] today, sixty years on, they would be bound to have extremely mixed feelings and it would be unsettling.

On the morning of 17 August, I finally reached Ningbo airport. When the 'plane landed I saw Mr Jordan walking with difficulty and was a bit worried for him. To tell the truth, at that time I had a heavy heart and was feeling some intangible pressure. I wondered what we should do for an elderly man of eighty-seven if this journey were to evoke many unhappy memories for him, and cause him to be upset when visiting the site? Or what if he was dissatisfied with the arrangements for the journey, what should I do: a guilty conscience, regrets...

On the way from Ningbo airport to Zhoushan City I saw old Mr Jordan constantly looking out of the window, looking at the scenery all around with a face like that of a happy child in a play park. I relaxed straightaway. This was the first time they had actually set foot on Chinese soil.[82] In Mr Jordan's case this was the first time he had personally experienced a peaceful China. In the memories he had kept for sixty years China was impoverished, backward, full of battlefield gun-smoke.

The year 2005 was the commemoration of the sixtieth anniversary of victory in the War of Resistance against Japan. Before the Jordan family and the Donald sisters set out, they attended many War of Resistance commemorative events in Hong Kong, including laying a wreath at the Cenotaph in Central District, attending an exhibition in the Central Library and so on. Every day Mr Jordan was interviewed by members of the press. This was probably useful preparation, as after he arrived in Zhoushan, he would inevitably be pursued by the local press as a target for interview.

After our group arrived in Zhoushan, a succession of friendship formalities began. However, the heavy workload involved gave me a fright, and also the reason I felt embarrassed was that, before setting out, he had no understanding of how enthusiastic the response of the Chinese media friends would be: for the whole journey the Chinese press were following him closely and interviewing him, which probably led to him becoming worn out throughout the journey.

Originally, I had a kind of intuitive idea about old Mr Jordan, I thought that he would complain to the press that as a veteran soldier of that time he had risked his life to defend a place he didn't know and a people he didn't know, and nearly paid for it with his life. So far as I was concerned, this was a rational view. However, throughout old Mr Jordan's entire visit, not only did he not complain of being tired on the journey, he also did not complain of the suffering he had personally experienced. Old Mr Jordan had come all the way from England to express his gratitude. Gratitude that had remained in his heart for sixty years. The feeling I got during the process of interpreting for him was that he was extremely grateful for everything the elderly Zhoushan fishermen had done more than sixty years before for him and his comrades who survived.

During this visit, the most moving scene for me and everyone was when he cast fresh flowers for the victims of the disaster on the open sea off Dongji Island in the area where the *Lisbon Maru* had gone down. On 2 October 1942, old Mr Jordan and the other 1,816[83] British prisoners of war were on board the *Lisbon Maru* which was sunk by a torpedo from an American submarine whilst en route to Japan. Amongst them nearly 1,000 of their close friends were killed; Mr Jordan was amongst the small number of lucky ones who were saved by the fishermen of Zhoushan. Most of those who died were either not saved, or drowned having given up all hope after their final desperate struggles…

We reached Zhoushan on a burning hot August day; the weather was scorching, and it was the season when typhoons cause havoc. Two weeks earlier, Typhoon Matsa had struck a surprise direct hit along the coast of Zhejiang Province. Dongji Island faces the Pacific Ocean, and all the houses and roads had been damaged or destroyed; so before setting out we were very concerned about the weather conditions in the area. However, today was a very important day for Dongji Island. No matter whether it was old Mr Jordan's family and the Donald sisters, the elderly fishermen who had saved the allied prisoners of war at the time, the vast numbers of the citizens of Zhoushan, the media from all parts of China … and of course the souls of those in the depths of the oriental ocean who drowned in the sea sixty-three years earlier. Having to wait for sixty-three years for the return visit of the quiet comrade-in-arms and his relatives really was too long.

Life is full of coincidences. 18 August 2005 was the fourteenth day of the seventh month of the lunar calendar, which is the Chinese traditional ghost festival. It is the time every year when the gates of hell are opened. However, at this time the sea was calm and tranquil, the sunlight was dazzling, with a light breeze blowing, causing people to feel this was a most beautiful tourist seascape. Listening to what the island fishermen said, Dongji Island gets this type of beautiful weather no more than twenty days a year. When we reached Dongji Island, fishermen on the shore were beating gongs and drums to welcome the honoured guests from a long way away. In consideration of the advanced years of these elderly people, the welcoming ceremony was simple and subdued. Young Pioneers presented fresh flowers to old Mr Jordan, the Donald sisters and the Hong Kong veteran soldier Mr Billy Wong Chi-hon. The Mayor, Mr Wang Hongbo, made a welcoming address, after which there was a meeting with the elderly fishermen of the time. With the remorseless passing of the years, many of those who took part in the events of the time have gone forever, and those left behind are already grey-haired old men. I should offer my thanks, there are too many things to feel grateful for, but after old Mr Jordan had shaken hands one by one with several of the elderly fishermen who were still in good health, he tightly embraced one individual. This affectionate embrace was better than a thousand words. This was unexpected as far as the eighty-year-old Chinese fisherman was concerned, who could not help showing that he was rather taken aback. However, here and now, so far as old men who lived under different cultures, languages and skin colour and yet who retained identical memories were concerned, this was the best way of expressing their feelings even though it was sixty-three years after the event.[84]

On leaving Dongji Island, old Mr Jordan was at a loss for words over his sense of comfort and pleasure. Perhaps it was the warm-hearted treatment by the Dongji fishermen, perhaps it was thinking again about the sweet potatoes and rice gruel that the Dongji fishermen had cooked for the starving prisoners of war. The steamship slowly left Dongji and headed for the sea where the *Lisbon Maru* had sunk, to perform a maritime ceremony of offering flowers for the victims of the disaster. When we reached the area of the sea where the sinking took place, old Mr Jordan stood silently at the stern, first lightly kissed the red rose in his hand, and prayed quietly, as if to give blessings to the comrades in arms who had shared adversity sixty-three years previously. Old Mr Jordan slowly cast the rose onto the surface of the *Lisbon Maru* waters. After that the Donald sisters gave a Scottish flag that they had brought specially from the UK for the soldiers of the Royal Scots Regiment who had perished on the ship, two of whom were their uncles. The Donald sisters made me think of a Chinese saying, "A gift may be as light as a goose feather, but sent from afar it conveys deep feeling". Others on board and we young Hong Kong friends all witnessed this moment, and one after another cast the flowers in our hands into the sea, to offer collective blessings to people from a foreign land who will remain in China forever.

As the ship sailed back, the sea remained calm and tranquil. On the small narrow ferry steamer, apart from the rumbling of the ship's engine, everything seemed quiet. Old Mr Jordan, an old man of eighty-seven years, had experienced the cruel war years, had experienced parting forever, had experienced a moment of the most selfless human courage; the lines on his face recorded the numerous storms he had encountered in the past. However, on this occasion he hung his head and shed a few tears. At this point I was unable to understand what was in old Mr Jordan's heart. Was he weeping with joy for his own rescue, or crying for his comrades-in-arms who had died? His young son Richard gently hugged his father and gently stroked his back, just like his father used to comfort him when he was young. That Mr Jordan had such a devoted son caused me to feel that family bonds don't distinguish between race, nationality or nations. "There's no difference between the drops of water from the eaves." You reap what you sow.

At this moment, the rapacious press photographers agreed to forego invading the private space of Mr Jordan and his son with camera flashes and the clicking of shutters for this scene.

Old Mr Jordan said he had returned to the UK after the war, and married his girlfriend who had waited for him for many years, Now he had five children and ten grandsons. His children were all successful and could make a useful contribution to society. It was only because the brave Zhoushan fishermen had rescued him that he was now able to have a beautiful happy family. Otherwise everything would have been just a hope. If there had been no war, his close friends on the *Lisbon Maru* or those from either side in the war who died, would like him have been able to build a happy family and lead a happy life.

The entire visit was only four very short days, but learning from experience brings out the loftiest sentiments in mankind. Whilst I was chatting with Mr Jordan's two sons Alan and Richard during the send-off of Mr Jordan and the Donald sisters, they described what they most valued from the visit. They said that not only had it enabled their father to successfully release the pent up emotions that had been buried deep in his heart for the past sixty-three years, bringing reminiscences and blessings for his comrades in arms, but they could also tell the next generation about their father's complex experiences and the kindness of Chinese people, and continue to make a contribution to the friendship between the Chinese and British people. And at the same time Alan said to me that he hoped we young friends from Hong Kong, having witnessed this historic event, would carry this message of peace to all people, to warn the new generation of young people to cherish peace. If we didn't draw lessons from the suffering experienced sixty years ago, then this journey to Zhoushan would have been in vain.

I acted as Mr Jordan's interpreter on this journey. Although I studied languages in England, my interpreting work was very unprofessional, in particular the effectiveness of my interpreting of Mandarin was barely satisfactory. Also I hadn't realised there would be so many media interviews, so the completion of Mr Jordan's visit was like having a weight lifted off my shoulders, but there was also a little self-reproof: in fact I could have done better. Before the visit was over, when we returned to the hotel after the farewell dinner, Mr Jordan and his family kindly came up to me, shaking hands one by one, and posing for a group photograph; they said, "This trip would not have been possible without you." So I made a small contribution to society!

(2) **Shirley Chun**

The *Lisbon Maru* Incident was a very special event because foreign troops were captured by Japanese soldiers in Hong Kong, sunk by an American submarine in Chinese waters and afterwards saved by Dongji fishermen. This incident, which could not be considered a major one, drew in four different major powers which at that time was a rare event, but no importance was attached to this incident, and it was gradually forgotten by the world. Perhaps in the annals of modern warfare, the *Lisbon Maru*, whose sinking led to the death of more than a thousand officers and soldiers, does not stand very high in the scale of casualties in incidents of terror. Perhaps even more people have been killed in even more brutal ways in many incidents. But it's very clear that in the *Lisbon Maru* Incident this was an unnecessary sacrifice. The failure of the Japanese army to rescue the prisoners of war who originally could have been rescued led to the death of more than a thousand officers and soldiers. This was a lack of respect for life by the Japanese soldiers, devoid of humanity.

This is the history of the *Lisbon Maru* Incident, it is something that has gradually been forgotten by people, but history does not forget. Even though I am a liberal arts student studying history, in the history course my teacher never mentioned this piece of history – whether it seemed large or small – perhaps even my teacher did not know of this incident?

Now, because I am doing the Hong Kong Awards for Young People Gold Level test, I attended the "Probing into the *Lisbon Maru* Incident" activities. This event was to me the greatest inspiration and reflection since I began studying.

The day before setting out for Zhoushan, I had already met Charles R Jordan, one of the *Lisbon Maru* survivors, and his family, and the two sisters Maureen and Sophia. The day I accompanied them on a visit to Shamshuipo,[85] the Jordan family and the two sisters gave me a good impression. Although they could not be considered young, and Mr Jordan was already over eighty years old, they were like small children walking up and down looking at things, and they also talked with great wit and humour, often making jokes with us. They absolutely did not have the seriousness of elderly people. The first day I was not affected by the miserable history of Mr Jordan's background.

The first day we arrived in Zhoushan, I still had the mindset of a tourist, but by the second day when we went to Dongji Island, my thinking completely turned around. I believe the others on the visit would confirm that this was the day that left the deepest impression; and I'm no exception. Wrapped in a clear bright curtain of rain, above the blue waves of the East China Sea, we stepped onto Dongji Island lit by the first glimmer of dawn and listened attentively to the moving story of sacrifice and the heroic rescue of British prisoners of war. Tying up at the site of the sinking sixty-three years ago, we thought of the souls of the hundreds of British prisoners of war whose bodies were buried beneath the sea. Our hearts were heavy.

"The ship's bow ploughed through ten thousand blue waves; the stern tossed up ten thousand pear blossoms." Accompanied by officials from Dongji Town and Zhoushan City, we reached

Dongji Island and attended the welcoming ceremony. On the boat journey to Dongji Island, Mr Jordan gave non-stop interviews to the local press. His answers were repetitive, but the reporters were still not fed up with questioning him over and over again. I saw that Mr Jordan was beginning to feel very tired and sleepy, and was also feeling increasingly uneasy at setting foot again at this place which had given him a second life.

When we got to Dongji Island we got a warm welcome from the local people. And I also began to feel touched like the British soldiers had felt that year at the warm reception they had received from the Zhoushan fishermen. Meeting once again the saviours of that year, although they could not communicate through speaking, one simple action is better than thousands of words. Mr Jordan's memories of that year – his not knowing what to do when the *Lisbon Maru* sank, his gratitude at being rescued, his being moved by the Dongji fishermen spontaneously offering gifts – all rushed into his head at the same moment. All sorts of feelings welled up in his heart. Even though I was watching at a distance from the side, I could still feel it.

On Dongji Island, after we had eaten, Mr Jordan and the others attended a welcoming ceremony, whilst our group of students went sight-seeing all over Dongji Island, helping me get a better understanding of this place, Dongji. The fishermen of Dongji Town showed great enthusiasm for everything. They were honest and simple, with the pronounced flavours of fishing village and local countryside. They would throw themselves into anything, most unlike Hong Kong people. They were easily satisfied, proud of their own way of life. I was especially surprised at the maturity of the developing oil painting art of their lifestyle, which was a further expression of their deep affection for their way of life. And I couldn't help admiring their attitude in rescuing people from the sunken ship without racial discrimination. In the war environment, to the Zhoushan fishermen their own survival was in doubt. Their own future was uncertain, and yet they chose to rescue others. They would rather save people's lives than pick up foreign goods floating on the sea; they would rather have hungry stomachs and let the British eat their fill. They gave the clothes off their backs to the British to ward off the cold. They knew the value of their own lives, but still bravely put their own safety completely aside for the British. This is the virtuous nature of the Zhoushan people, compassion stored deep in their innermost hearts.

Although after the event the Zhoushan fishermen rejected society's high praise, and their heroic actions gradually faded from their memories, and they thought only of maintaining their simple, hard-working lifestyle, yet history should not forget them. Their selfless spirit still survives today in the hearts of every Zhoushan person, whose utterly unaffected warmth towards us left me with a deep sense of how moved the British soldiers were when they were given a warm reception by the Zhoushan fishermen that year. It's like the feeling of an unexpected encounter with an old friend, "providing timely help following one disaster after another". This is not only praise for the citizens of Zhoushan, even more this is something we need to study.

Leaving Dongji Island, we neared the place where the *Lisbon Maru* had gone down: at 122° 45' 55" East, 30° 30' 37" North. All around was the vast ocean, but when the boat slowly came to a stop, it was as if the *Lisbon Maru* Incident of that year was reappearing before our eyes: the terrifying torpedo strike, the panic-stricken British prisoners of war, the hearts of the prisoners getting gradually colder as the *Lisbon Maru* was slowly sinking. This stretch of vast and deep ocean staged the performance in that year sixty-three years ago, and I believe it was being played out again in Mr Jordan's mind. That day was 18 August 2005, the 14th day of the 7th month in the solar calendar,[86] the Chinese ghost festival; Zhoushan City reserved this day to hold a memorial ceremony to mourn the souls of the 843[87] British who had been buried at the bottom of the sea at that time. Flowers were presented by Mr Jordan and family, the two sisters Maureen and Sophia and our group of youths. After presenting the flowers, Mr Jordan could not bear the deep sorrow in his heart and tears fell ceaselessly. At that time it was easy to see that Mr Jordan was clearly shouldering a very grave historic burden. When I presented the flowers, other than praying that they could rest in peace, I could not help sighing with regret: if the Japanese had planned that year to rescue those British prisoners of war and not treated their lives with indifference and decided not to rescue them, the world would have a thousand more lucky families like

Mr Jordan's. The actions of the Japanese that year were undoubtedly inhumane actions, which made me feel even more disgusted by Japanese militarism.

Originally I had known only fragments of the Second World War. The experience of this visit to Dongji gave me shock after shock. To get a good understanding takes more than just skill and observation, even more important is to consolidate the experience of former people, and get an holistic view of the entire incident. If you want to know history and want to know the price of peace, you should carry out heartfelt reflection using history as a mirror, to understand why Japan up to now still obstinately sticks to a wrong course, firmly believing in their own terrifying actions that year. They don't hesitate to distort history and still want to blunt popular education.

But history is always impartial. Because it cannot tell lies, the public will know, because justice is in people's hearts. This is just like a sentence I saw in the [Hong Kong] Museum of Maritime Defence, which I won't be able to forget for a long time, "They shall grow not old, as we that are left grow old; Age shall not weary them, nor the years condemn; At the going down of the sun and in the morning, We will remember them." – Robert Laurence Binyon (1869-1943).

At the same time, I also want to let great numbers of citizens know of these deeds. Not only the elderly can strive to cherish past events, even more, young people can understand more historic events of that year. It's not purely eat, drink and be merry, blindly following foreign fashion, but they can use history as a mirror, for a deeper level of understanding of things in the modern world and reflect on this, "By correctly and objectively analysing this piece of history, you will value this piece of history even more." I hope that these events will not pass with time. I hope that people of the world can know about these historic events, know that that year there was a group of people who quietly, heroically sacrificed themselves to defend our Hong Kong, enabling us on today's 60th anniversary of the War of Resistance to stand in silent tribute and thank them for everything they did for Hong Kong.

(3) **Hei Ng**

During this seven-day journey we spent some time with and became friendly with the veteran Mr Jordan and his family as well as Maureen and her sister, and we learned from their lips things about the Second World War and their feelings. I felt that I myself was getting close to history especially when we reached Dongji Island. That kind of feeling is difficult to put into words.

When I first saw Mr Jordan I was already very moved, because Mr Jordan was of advanced age and had still come all the way from England to Dongji Island in China with the aim of seeing the fishermen who had rescued him and to thank them. Seeing Mr Jordan's warmth and sincerity, I was genuinely very moved, and walking together with his wife and two sons I could see how warm, united, and of one mind the family were.

Although the two sisters, Maureen and Sophia, had not experienced the Second World War themselves, they had heard about their uncles' deeds and they very much wanted to say goodbye to their uncles. Furthermore, they also wanted to tell the next generation about this incident, in the hope that the next generation would know about the disasters brought by war.

During those few days, I understood that Chinese people, even people all over the world, paid close attention to mutually related incidents in the Second World War. I could see the great importance of this incident because every day our journey had many reporters conducting interviews and furthermore our reception was very good. I rejoiced that I was taking part in this trip because with this journey I was able to have the motive to push forward my own search for material and literature on the Second World War, and I had the opportunity to discuss directly the situation in that place during the Second World War with the two old soldiers Mr Jordan and Mr Billy Wong Chi-hon, especially Mr Billy Wong. He was one of the gunners garrisoned in Hong Kong in the Second World War, like Mr Jordan, under command of the Royal Artillery. He spoke a lot about what actually happened when the Japanese army invaded Hong Kong and how the Japanese army treated civilians. Although this material can be found in books, when I heard Mr Wong Chi-hon, who was involved, explaining from his own experience, that kind of earth-shattering and realistic feeling is not something you can get from books.

The second day was the day that affected me the deepest, because you could say that was the focal point of the whole visit – Dongji Island. Dongji Island, as the name implies, is China's most easterly small island[88], so early in the morning we took the boat to our destination. We talked for a long time with Mr Jordan and his family and Maureen and her sister during the several hours on the boat. Whilst talking to them I felt their kindness, as they could talk to us about everything under the sun, even sharing their personal affairs with us just as if we were old friends. They did not avoid us at all; they also discussed their views about the Second World War. The aim of this visit, apart from accompanying Mr Jordan, was also to photograph the entire incident, and return home so that the next generation would understand.

I also very much agreed with their thinking. I was not born when the Second World War broke out, so I knew absolutely nothing about the War, and school also could not talk about this aspect of history, perhaps because the cost of the Second World War has gradually been disregarded. No-one talks about war any more, especially in the peaceful world of today. But it is precisely because we want to safeguard peace that it is really important to tell the younger generation about the reasons for the Second World War and its effects. Only then will our generation be able to understand the importance and value of peace, and enable us – even though our strength is puny – to make every effort to protect peace. This is what I learned from Mr Jordan's family and Maureen and her sister.

On the boat, we also chatted with one of the fishermen who had taken part in the rescue that year. He said that when they saw the *Lisbon Maru* which had been attacked and had sunk, they had no second thoughts about rescuing people from the sea. At the time they had rowed out to rescue them, and in the end rescued more than 300, and they even helped three high ranking soldiers to escape capture by the Japanese army. They absolutely did not know the soldiers on board the *Lisbon Maru*, and also their rescue equipment at the time was very simple and crude, but they still went to the aid of the victims of the sunken ship regardless of the consequences. I was genuinely very moved. Furthermore they said they did not rescue people for any advantage, but out of good intentions. This is very hard to find in the materialistic society we live in. Even up to now, I am still affected by the fishermen's honesty and sincerity when I was on Dongji Island. This is really admirable.

When we reached Dongji Island, the fishermen there received us warmly. Mr Jordan's visit was really important to them, because this was a glorious event on their island. At the reception, when I saw Mr Jordan and the fisherman who had rescued him embracing, how magnificent and genuine was the smile on Mr Jordan's face. From the side I could still feel Mr Jordan's happiness and be affected by Mr Jordan's sense of gratitude. Regardless of the language communication difficulty and the difference in nationality, there was a wholehearted exchange, and he put across the most sincere and profound gratitude.

In the afternoon, our group took a boat to the place where the *Lisbon Maru* had gone down, and offered flowers to those who had died. After Mr Jordan had offered a flower, he wept. I felt his tears contained grief, and were full of cherished memories. He passed on his feelings through the rose to his comrades who had been with him at that time on the *Lisbon Maru*. I shall never be able to forget that scene.

Maureen and her sister also offered flowers. They too were involved because their uncles, whom they had never met, had taken part in the Second World War. When they heard about the *Lisbon Maru* Incident they wanted to go there and feel history and also bid farewell to their uncles. And whilst at first you could say I knew absolutely nothing about the Second World War, through the experience of this visit my knowledge of the Second World War became deeper and deeper. I believe this was an opportunity.

I also think that if I had not taken part in this visit, I would not have been able to take the initiative to understand the Second World War. This lets me think about whether our young generation have thought about the events of the previous two generations? The Second World War was only sixty years before our time, yet surprisingly we know nothing about it. History textbooks can teach the history of ancient times; on the other hand, why can a course not be made on the Second World War, which was less than 100 years ago? Even though we know about the Second World War history, can we understand history as energetically as Maureen and her sister? This point makes me feel ashamed of myself.

Finally our group of young people also offered flowers to the sea. The instant I cast the flowers in my hand into the sea, the history I had seen in books appeared in my mind, although I had not taken part in the Second World War, and had never seen the young men on the *Lisbon Maru*. I felt that we should treasure the fact that we were now placed in a peaceful age; we should be sure to cherish everything about today, and not follow again the ruinous path of the Second World War. This flower offering ceremony really affected me a great deal, and was also the scene which gave me the deepest impression on this trip.

After the journey we also got on well with Mr Jordan's family, Maureen and her sister and Billy Wong Chi-hon, and I learned a great deal directly from them. Not only knowledge of the Second World War, but even other history, and also how to get along with other people. Because of this I was very happy that I was able to take part in this trip, not only because of the richness of the course,[89] but also because I was able to take part in historic activities, broaden my own vision, and it was even more important to understand the consequences war brings and the value of peace.

(4) **Polly Poon**

The first I knew of this Incident was from what we learned when we attended the "Three Days Two Nights Hong Kong Battlefield Study" in Hong Kong. What we knew was superficial. Only afterwards, when we took part in the visit to Dongji, were we able to travel in person to the site of this historic incident.

During this trip, there were some people who gave me the deepest impression and the deepest feelings.

The first was Mr Jordan. The impression Mr Jordan gave me was of a very kind old man, with a kindly smile on his face. At first I really did not understand actually how great had been the influence on him of the sinking of the *Lisbon Maru*, until the day we went to the site of the *Lisbon Maru* to offer flowers. Mr Jordan was not the same as usual that day. His appearance became more serious than before, perhaps because he was recalling again what happened at that time, and remembering his comrades in arms. I very much remember that after Mr Jordan offered a flower he could not hold back his tears.

And I thought that this war must be one of the main reasons for Mr and Mrs Jordan being so much in love. During the course of the several days visit to Dongji, Mr Jordan was meticulous in his attentions to his wife. Wherever they went, Mr Jordan would hold his wife's hand. When he finished an interview elsewhere, the first thing he did was to look for his wife. I particularly remember that when we were going to Dongji, Mr Jordan gave his wife an affectionate kiss in front of our group. I thought that this kiss, as well as containing love, was also gratitude to his wife. Speaking for myself, although war is very brutal and merciless, and also many families are broken up because of war, yet at the same time, war also teaches us how to cherish – cherish the people and things around us; cherish a life of peace. And also because he had experienced war, Mr Jordan understood even more that he should cherish everything.

The second was the Dongji fishermen. If there had not been at that time this group of fishermen who rescued British soldiers from the sea, perhaps we would not be having this journey. Although this group of fishermen were completely uneducated and had lived their entire lives on this small island, when they saw people floating on the sea, without a thought they rescued them, and one of those they rescued was Mr Jordan. I remember on Dongji Island, seeing Mr Jordan and the fisherman who rescued him embracing for a moment, I could feel deeply Mr Jordan's gratitude to the fisherman, because if this fisherman had not been there, Mr Jordan long ago would not have been in this world. Just because of this fisherman's selfless rescue, not only did Mr Jordan not die during the Incident, he now also enjoyed a happy family. I think the fishermen's selfless spirit should be something worth our learning from, because if everyone only considered themselves, the world would change to one lacking humanity and relations between people would become more and more cold and detached. And when I stepped on Dongji Island, the Island people welcomed us very warmly, gave us the best reception and the best food. They just set us an example. If in the future Dongji people come to Hong Kong we should also give them the best reception.

Although the Donald sisters were not veteran soldiers, they also gave me much food for thought. We interviewed the pair on the boat: what caused them to be so set on making the long arduous journey to come out here? They said, because their uncles had been lost in this war, on the one hand they hoped to come themselves to be able to offer flowers and express thanks to their uncles and other soldiers who had died a hero's death, and on the other hand they hoped to learn more about the Incident. Their conduct left me full of admiration. They decided to abandon their settled lifestyle and from faraway Scotland come to a strange country, all because of an incident of history. As a Hong Kong person, I really felt ashamed. At that time, Hong Kong was invaded by Japan. A group of British troops struggled for us, and they were taken onto the *Lisbon Maru* only because of Hong Kong. So I believe it's even more important that Hong Kong people should know more about this Incident and express gratitude to that group of soldiers.

This journey was the first time I had personally come into contact with history; come into contact with this war. War is really very frightening and the disasters it brings are really too many, but because I have seen[90] the terror of war, I cherish even more today's peace and everything we have at present. And if there is an opportunity, I would really like to be able to come here again for the 70th Anniversary of the War of Resistance against Japan. When I'm ten years older I will probably have more understanding about this Incident.

(5) **Wing Tang**

Starting with when I stepped onto that steamboat going to Dongji Island, it is actually difficult to describe the excitement, even though we knew it was going to take about six hours on the boat to get there.

I still remember at that time I was constantly thinking what will be there? Are the people there like us? What's it like? What about the people's lifestyle?...A large heap of questions immediately sprang up. Thinking back on it now, it's really funny.

Since the guide who brought us, Guide Shum,[91] had already told us something of the background to the place, everyone had already prepared themselves for its strangeness.

On the boat, through interviewing every crew member and fisherman who had experienced being affected by the fire of war at that time, our understanding of the environment of the stretch of water near Dongji Island was deepened, and one by one the deeds – such as the fishermen at that time taking old soldiers to a place of safety and thus avoiding capture by the Japanese soldiers – were clarified, so that we understood the urgency at that time. When we saw the fishermen explaining to us the situation at that time, it was like feeling history before our eyes, it was really distressing! And we also interviewed Mr and Mrs Jordan, their two sons and the Donald sisters, and they all gave their different feelings. Amongst these what left the deepest impression was the love expressed by Mr and Mrs Jordan. Apart from being deeply in love with each other, they loved their sons, their friends, and also us – people who had no connection with their sufferings – they also loved, and expressed such warmth towards.

After we had reached our destination, it was really "unlike anything else before". That is to say, we had never before seen so many people come out to welcome us. Originally all the villagers from the entire village performed probably their first welcoming ceremony, and furthermore they had also not seen so many people arrive on their island. Moreover they said they had never before seen Hong Kong people so close, they had only seen them on television, and actually this is what Hong Kong people are like.

Ha, they are so cute!

On the island, after the simple and grand welcoming ceremony was over, we ate a complete seafood feast, then went out to begin to get to know something about the island. On the way we saw that all the villagers gazed at us very strangely; it felt very odd.

We had originally planned to stay on the island for one night, but after sightseeing, although we did not want to go, we left Dongji Island, the fear being that since the earlier typhoon[92] had just devastated this island, we could not stay overnight, therefore for safety reasons, we had to change our plans.

Mr Jordan (back to the photographer) and Hong Kong students, who followed the elderly gentleman to Zhoushan to conduct on-site historical research, attended the welcoming dinner given by Zhoushan local Party and government organisations.

On the journey back, our large group all went to the area where the *Lisbon Maru* had sunk to hold a memorial ceremony for the victims. I still remember seeing Mr Jordan picking up the fresh flowers, and after lightly kissing the rose meditating for a while and then throwing it. He immediately went to one side and shed tears on the site. His son went over to console him. That moment was very heart-rending. On the other side, the Donald sisters had prepared a home-made national flag to offer to their uncles and cast it into the sea together with the roses. Afterwards, everyone separately went forward and took the fresh flowers, and standing in silent tribute cast them into the ocean....

The telling of Hong Kong's history – including the historical material of the 18-day defence of Hong Kong and the three years and eight months of enemy occupation of Hong Kong – is far from complete, and Hong Kong students study local history in the classroom. The *Lisbon Maru* Incident, this tiny interlude in the Second World War, with its thousands of millions of casualties, could easily be forgotten by the world.

Perhaps, as far as our generation who never took part in war nor went through hardships is concerned, it's nothing very serious. We don't even understand the value of happiness, but wantonly squander it. But, when you go to the area where the ship sank to hold a memorial service and grieve, and react to seeing again the people of that time, you won't be able to help weeping, because sixty-three years after the War, going back by yourself to the battlefield and lamenting the day when brothers-in-arms lived and died together, how heart-breaking it is, recalling that terrifying war. Now, only yourself still surviving in this world, even though accompanied by family members, considering the wounds and after-effects brought by that war, how many people would be able to understand the sadness of this?

Therefore, this trip to Dongji taught me to cherish the present and look forward to the future, and I also learned from Mr Jordan and the fishermen to understand that we should "live in the moment".

A vivid education
Zhoushan Daily: reporters Chen Yafang and Ni Ligang[93]

Yesterday, a group of Hong Kong students followed a British military survivor of the *Lisbon Maru* disaster and his relatives on a visit to Dongji. They said this was a vivid education.

Amongst the visiting group with the *Lisbon Maru* disaster survivor and his relatives there was also a group of Hong Kong secondary students, in their early teens. They were extremely active.

So far as these children were concerned, from a young age they have grown up in bustling Hong Kong: peaceful, where war is a strange and remote term. But so as to let these children be aware of past humiliation and treasure the beautiful life of today, the Hong Kong Buddhist Association Children and Youth Centre Programme Secretary Mr Kent Shum, acting as a go-between, organised these secondary school students to come to Zhoushan, to find out about the deeds of the Dongji fishermen who saved lives and experienced the Japanese atrocity.

Jau Chiu-yan is a seventeen-year-old Hong Kong True Light Middle School Grade Five (senior grade Two in Mainland China) student and has grown to have a very fair complexion. She was wearing a pink T-shirt and jeans and appeared very relaxed. She was very softly spoken. Standing beside her, wearing a tooth brace, was Hoh Bo-yi, the same age as her, who came from the same school and the same year.

"We took part in a 'witnessing poverty' activity, mainly investigating countries invaded by Japan during the Second World War. This was the first time we had come to Zhoushan and we were moved by the actions of the Dongji fishermen in saving British soldiers, and being able to go to the site where the *Lisbon Maru* sank and pay respects to the victims was extremely significant," Hoh Bo-yi told reporters.

When the boat was going to the area where the *Lisbon Maru* had sunk, the students who had not previously experienced large waves and wind were a bit seasick. But when they cast flowers at the memorial service for the victims, everyone of them was particularly solemn and serious.

Children and Youth Centre Secretary Mr Kent Shum,
photographed with an elderly fisherman,
believes that educating the next generation by personal exposure to history
has greater practical significance than the contents of text books.

"In the Hong Kong Award for Young People there is a hiking requirement; getting us to walk over all the hills in Hong Kong, walking again along the line of the Japanese invasion of Hong Kong in that year," said Jau Chiu-yan.

Mr Kent Shum said, "Reviewing history, educating children, is not confined to text books. Integrating teaching into travel lets children learn themselves through practice. It's more vivid, more profound.

Elderly Zhoushan fishermen visit Hong Kong
Zhoushan Daily[94]

Looking into the distance from high up in the Hong Kong Special Administrative Region, Victoria Harbour seems unusually tranquil. In 1942, the Japanese packet ship *Lisbon Maru* set sail carrying 1,816[95] British prisoners of war from the Shamshuipo concentration camp. Five days later, she arrived in the area of the Zhoushan waters. Because it had no markings to show it was carrying prisoners of war, it was hit by a torpedo fired from the American submarine USS *Grouper*. On the edge of life and death, fishermen from Dongji, Zhoushan, risking the threat of discovery by the Japanese Army, resolutely went ahead to carry out a rescue.

In 2005, elderly Zhoushan fishermen who had taken part in rescuing British prisoners of war visited Hong Kong and were received personally by Hong Kong entrepreneur Mr Henry Fok who is Vice Chairman of the Chinese People's Political Consultative Conference and is known as a "patriotic businessman".

At about 4.00pm on 16 June 2005 an aircraft from Ningbo flew to Hong Kong and gently landed at Hong Kong International Airport. Shen Agui, Lin Fuyun, Chen Yonghua, Wang Baoce and Wu Lanfang, elderly fishermen from Dongji who had personally rescued British prisoners of war that year, came on a visit to

Hong Kong at the invitation of the Second World War Veterans' Association, organised by the Zhoushan Municipal *Lisbon Maru* Incident Historical Research Association.

From Zhoushan to Hong Kong is a journey of over a thousand kilometres; but the flight takes only half a day. However, the British Army officers and soldiers who were victims on the *Lisbon Maru* have already been sleeping in Zhoushan waters for sixty-three years. During the five-day visit, members of the visiting group used their own experience and related historical material to tell people about the breath-taking historic incident that took place in Dongji, Zhoushan. This was the authentic reappearance of the internationalist and humanitarian spirit of the people of Zhoushan and even of the whole nation.

Chairman of the British Chamber of Commerce Brig Christopher Hammerbeck pictured with elderly fishermen[96]

On the evening of the 16 June, the Second World War Veterans' Association held a grand ceremony in the Chinese Recreation Club, Hong Kong, to welcome the group on their visit to Hong Kong. Mr Henry Fok Ying-tung, Vice Chairman of the Chinese People's Political Consultative Conference and a Hong Kong celebrity, personally hurried to come to receive them, and praised highly the magnificent undertaking of the Zhoushan fishermen. Hong Kong Second World War Veterans' Association Chairman Mr Maximo Cheng and the British Chamber of Commerce Chairman Brig Christopher Hammerbeck held a friendly exchange with the visiting group, and presented members of the delegation and the elderly fishermen with mementos. The Hong Kong Underwater Association expressed a strong interest in going to explore under the Dongji waters. That day, also present were veteran Hong Kong soldiers who had taken part in the Second World War, and who conveyed to the elderly fishermen their expressions of the highest respect and sincere gratitude.

The elderly fishermen went to the Sai Wan War Cemetery and presented flowers for allied soldiers who were killed in action defending Hong Kong in the War.[97]

On 17 June the visiting group went to the site of the Shamshuipo concentration camp to have a look around. At that time this was a concentration camp imprisoning up to a thousand British prisoners of war. Now it is a clean and green park, with trees, birds singing, and fragrant flowers, allowing people to dismiss from their minds what happened here in the past. Then they went to the Sai Wan War Cemetery to present wreaths and grieve for the allied officers and soldiers killed in action in the Second World War. That afternoon, a "Zhoushan fishermen rescue British soldiers in the Second World War, and the first global exploration of the *Lisbon Maru*" press conference was held in the

Century Hong Kong Hotel. Hong Kong film stars Jackie Lui, Jessica Hsuan, McIntosh Ting and Kwok Fung made a special trip to "help out".

That evening and the next morning, more than twenty Hong Kong media outlets, such as the Hong Kong Special Administrative Region Branch of the *New China News Agency*, *Wenweipo*, *Asia TV* and *Global View*, reported the visit to Hong Kong and the events of the Dongji fishermen rescuing British officers and soldiers from the *Lisbon Maru*, creating interest amongst all sections of Hong Kong society.

From 18 to 20 June, the visiting group continued their visit to Hong Kong, and met Tony Banham, author of *The Sinking of the "Lisbon Maru": Britain's Forgotten Wartime Tragedy* and exchanged views on related matters. At midday on 20 June the visiting group completed their visit to Hong Kong and returned to Zhoushan.

Visiting group of elderly Dongji Fishermen impress Hong Kong
Zhoushan Daily: Reporter Chen Yafang[98]

The visiting group of elderly Dongji fishermen who rescued British prisoners of war during the Second World War and who arrived in Hong Kong on the afternoon of 16 June 2005, day after day received a warm welcome from people of the Hong Kong Special Administrative Region and became targets of pursuit by more than twenty media outlets.

Henry Fok, "You elderly fishermen are extraordinary!"

After Vice Chairman of the Chinese People's Political Consultative Conference heard the news that five elderly Dongji fishermen, including Chen Yonghua and Shen Agui, were visiting Hong Kong, despite his advanced years, he met them personally at the Chinese Recreation Club on the evening of 16th, and praised them for performing an extraordinary feat, which deserves very good publicity, to let people of the whole world know of the humanitarian spirit of the Zhoushan fishermen.

Recalling past events at the Shamshuipo concentration camp

On the morning of 17 June, five elderly Dongji fishermen and members of the "the Second World War Veterans' Association" went together to the site of the Hong Kong Shamshuipo concentration camp where the victims of the *Lisbon Maru* Incident had been imprisoned. It was there that 1,816[99] British prisoners of war had been escorted in 1942 on to the *Lisbon Maru* to be transported to Japan, but they never thought they were going from here on a one way trip. But for the magnanimous actions of the Zhoushan Dongji fishermen, they would all have been buried on the seabed.

Now, only three stone pillars with "Army Headquarters Boundary" engraved at the base remain on the site of the concentration camp of the time. The rest has been made into a park and a swimming pool. Only the trees in the park witnessed the crimes of the Japanese army.

Memorial ceremony in Sai Wan War Cemetery for the souls of those who died in the Second World War

In drizzle and fine rain, the elderly fishermen also went to the Sai Wan War Cemetery in Chai Wan to hold a memorial ceremony and present fresh flowers, to show their respect for the British officers and soldiers who were sacrificed in the War of Resistance or who died after being taken prisoner.

The Sai Wan War Cemetery has 1,578 graves, many of which only have the personal effects of the deceased, but no body. So as to remember these officers and soldiers whose burial place is unknown, the cemetery has a memorial plaque built at the entrance, engraved with the names of 2,071 soldiers who died for their country in the same period of time.

Film and TV stars pursue heroic fishermen

Hong Kong film stars, representing the Hong Kong film stars underwater team, pictured together with elderly fishermen.[100]

Jackie Lui, Jessica Hsuan, McIntosh Ting and Kwok Fung, these stars who are normally being pursued by others as targets, on the afternoon of 17 June at the "Zhoushan fishermen rescued British soldiers in the Second World War, and the first global exploration of the *Lisbon Maru*" press conference not only competed to present fresh flowers to the elderly fishermen, they also vied one after the other to have their pictures taken with the elderly fishermen as souvenirs.

In the Hong Kong production of *Swordsman*, Jackie Lui plays the hero Linghu Chong. This day he was a martial arts hero meeting real heroes. When being interviewed by reporters, the star Jessica Hsuan declared that this was an extremely significant event. This was the first time in her whole life she had been able to take part personally in an activity connected with history. Perhaps in August she would go to Dongji to explore the sunken *Lisbon Maru*.

Lisbon Maru: Dusty historical testimony
Zhejiang Daily: Reporters Xie Guoping and Shen Feilun[101]

At a meeting of the Zhoushan City Fourth People's Congress held in the first half of 2002, People's Congress delegate Wang Haigang, from Dongji Town in Putuo District, Zhoushan City, made a proposal to the Congress regarding a request to salvage the sunken Japanese ship *Lisbon Maru*. In his proposal, Wang Haigang wrote, "According to relevant material, the *Lisbon Maru* that year was carrying gold, silver and treasures plundered by the Japanese army from many places, and British prisoners of war. And when sailing in the waters of Qingbang Island, Dongji, Putuo, it was sunk by a torpedo. If the salvage is successful, we could establish a Second World War memorial museum and a monument, to act here as a patriotic educational base."

The raising of this proposal in Zhoushan created many waves, opening up dusty memories in the hearts of the island people. These were that in the early morning of 2 October 1942, a large ship flying a Rising Sun flag was sailing on the high seas in the direction away from Qingbang Island. As it passed Seven Seas at Qingbang Island, suddenly there was an earth-shattering noise, and a huge column of water shot up into the air. In an instant, the stern of the large ship sank "whoosh" into the ocean, and the bow rose up, a lot of people and goods on the ship fell into the vast ocean. Risking their lives to save others from the perils of the sea is a traditional virtue of the Zhoushan fishermen. When the Qingbang fishermen saw this scene, one after another they grabbed their oars and rowed their boats to where the incident had happened. Old Wang Awu's sampan crossed Swallow Bay and he saw a lot of blue-eyed blonde foreigners[102] in blue life-jackets, half floating, half sinking. Old Wang exerted all his strength to pull them one at a time out of the sea into his sampan. The faces of the foreigners who barely escaped with their lives showed feelings of gratitude, and they used hand signals and crude Chinese to tell the Qingbang fishermen that they were British officers and soldiers fighting shoulder to shoulder with the Chinese against the Japanese devils. They had been captured by the Japanese invaders in Hong Kong and were sailing to Japan on the Japanese ship *Lisbon Maru* when en route they had been sunk by a torpedo from a submarine. When the Qingbang Island fishermen heard that they were fighting the Japanese devils, they cared even less about the fast winds and large waves, and risked their lives to rescue them, altogether saving more than four hundred British officers and soldiers. But afterwards they learned that the number of people who died on the *Lisbon Maru* who had no time to escape and those who were engulfed by raging billows after falling into the water reached into the hundreds. Qingbang Island is an isolated island close to the dangerous waters of the high seas, with an area of only 1.45 square kilometres; there is not one paddy field on the island and only a small amount of sweet potatoes are grown on the hills. After the Japanese bandits invaded China, the isolated island was cut off from the outside and the islanders suffered extreme privations.

However, no matter how poor, they could not treat shabbily allied soldiers who were fighting the Japanese. The islanders took the British friends they had rescued into their homes and entertained their guests by serving them seafood such as jellyfish, conch dumplings and clams. A British soldier O'Neas thanked old Bian Deyun very much for his lavish hospitality and gave him as a present his own treasured ring for a souvenir, and afterwards Old Bian wore it on his finger.[103]

After two days, there was a rumbling sound in the air as several Black Raven Japanese aircraft flew over Qingbang Island, dropped bombs where the ship had sunk and strafed the area with machine-gun fire. On the morning of the fourth day, Qingbang Island was encircled by four or five Japanese ships with the pitch black muzzles of the guns pointing straight at the fishing village. The Japanese bandits, carrying gleaming bayonets, overbearingly kicked open the doors, smashed the houses, went from door to door, searching, and threatened that they were not to hide one British soldier. They wantonly hung up and beat the unarmed fishermen. The British soldiers had no alternative but were forced to put up their hands and line up together. When they were forced at bayonet point onto the Japanese ship, they repeatedly turned round and waved greetings to the fishermen to say goodbye.

After the more than four hundred British soldiers who had been rescued from the raging billows by the Qingbang Island fishermen and then taken prisoner again by the Japanese Army had been sent to Shanghai, they were escorted to Japanese prisoner-of-war concentration camps in Japan. They were looked after by the Red Cross from non-combatant nations such as Turkey, Portugal, Spain, Switzerland and Sweden. And only after the Japanese unconditional surrender were they able to return to the British Isles and be reunited with their families. On 27 February 1949, there was a solemn mourning in Hong Kong for the tragedy in which nearly two thousand British officers and soldiers on the Japanese ship *Lisbon Maru* lost their lives, and praise for the contributions of the fishermen of Qingbang Island in saving more than four hundred British soldiers who had fallen into the sea.

The government of Great Britain and Northern Ireland expressed its gratitude for the commendable humanity of the fishermen of Qingbang, Zhoushan, and through the Governor of Hong Kong, Sir Alexander Grantham, presented the fishermen of Qingbang with a steam boat for use as a communications boat. The spirit of life and death that cuts across national boundaries cannot be extinguished. After half a century, in December 1991, hundreds of British army officers and soldiers who had taken part in the defence of Hong Kong in the Second World War were invited to Hong Kong. Former British Indian Naval Lt Jim Fallace,[104] with a full head of white hair, arrived from Kent and spoke of his experience of being rescued in Zhoushan. Not only were his eyes brimming with tears, but he also really wanted to meet up once again with the benefactors of former days from Qingbang Island who had saved his life and talk with them to their hearts' content.

The years move on inexorably. Fishermen Weng Azhou and the others who rescued British prisoners of war have passed away one after the other. Originally the mast revealed the sea surface of the *Lisbon Maru*. Due to tidal currents and the changing topography of the seabed, it has completely fallen into oblivion, but the spirit of the *Lisbon Maru* and this piece of Sino-British friendship has taken root in the hearts of the people of Dongji. Up to now, there are still quite a few Dongji people who still keep the things given as presents by the British people that year.

In 1998 the Zhoushan City Liaison Committee, in coordination with the local town government, organised people to carry out a deep water exploration of the Qingbang sunken ship. According to the results of the exploration, determining the specific condition of the *Lisbon Maru*, it was considered to have a salvage value. Through the discovery made by the exploration, the sunken ship lies in twenty-seven metres of water at $122°$ 45'55" East and $30°13'48"$ North. The sunken ship is about 116 metres long and about eighteen metres broad. Wang Haigang said that, in line with the results of the examination, we can draft a first stage plan for salvage.

Qingbang Fishing Village on Qingbang Island[105]

Wang Haigang made a proposal that the city government should get a specialist salvage company to use a fifty metric-ton crane ship and other advanced equipment apparatus, to record every item salvaged, compile a register and put them into storage. A faithful record should be archived of the accounts provided by some of the fishermen who rescued British officers and soldiers at the time, and furthermore the utensils left behind by the British officers and soldiers that year, some of the historical artefacts recovered from the salvaged ship, as well as material from underwater photographs, should be used as an important foundation for analysis and research on the ship before breaking out the cargo, to supply important historic material for the Second World War Memorial Hall which the government will set up in future.

The department concerned in Zhoushan City took this proposal very seriously, and are currently undertaking the first phase of the research and analysis preparatory work for the salvage. Dongji Town is furthermore taking this as a turning point in the rapid development of island tourism, exerting itself to unearth the politics, culture and economic connotations of this incident. Known as the "The Extreme East Land in the Sea", Dongji Town is formed from the four inhabited islands of Miaozihu, Qingbang, Huangxing, Dongfushan, [106] close to the high seas, the most extreme easterly inhabited islands in the open sea along China's southeast coast. Here people are honest and simple. Fishing families have strong affection. There is an abundance of natural resources such as the islands, reefs and caves; the seascape and mountain scenery are beautiful and these gifts of nature provide the conditions for developing tourism. Therefore, the town is keen to build Dongji into a bright and beautiful monument to international humanitarianism and a famous scenic resort.

In October 2002, on the occasion of the 60th Anniversary of Dongji fishermen rescuing British army victims in the Second World War, the post office printed more than 2,600 commemorative mail covers as a public issue, to mark the life-and-death friendship between the British and Chinese military and civilians, recalling the memories that have gradually faded from people's minds, revisiting "ancient battlefields in extreme places". The town also set up the Zhoushan Dongji *Lisbon Maru* Research Society, made up of relevant people such as historians, old soldiers and elderly locals, to conduct thorough research and enquiries into the *Lisbon Maru* Incident.

The Dongji Town Government went to Beijing to convene a seminar on the 60th Anniversary of Zhoushan Dongji fishermen rescuing British army victims in the Second World War and invited famous scholars, experts and cultural figures in Beijing to hold informal discussions, to reveal this mysterious piece of history and comfort the spirits of the thousand British victims who have long been sleeping on the Dongji ocean floor. With the Dongji Town Government acting as an intermediary, the local area also set up a Zhoushan *Lisbon Maru* Oceanic Cultural Company, responsible for planning, management and marketing.

Currently, the *Lisbon Maru* Incident has been adapted into a film script. The film studio concerned is actively consulting Dongji Town, preparing to film the incident as a sister film to "Titanic", to show again this moving and tragic historic scene.

Secretary of the Dongji Town Party Committee and Mayor Jiang Xiding said, "The wreck of the *Lisbon Maru* is a treasure store, we must utilise, develop and apply properly these historical riches very close to us."

Nineteen-Year-Old Shen Agui rescued seven Britons
Zhejiang Online: Reporter Li Min[107]

Before Typhoon Matsa arrived, as the site reporter I visited the eastern extremity of Zhoushan, Dongji Township in the Zhongjieshan chain of islands. During the enquiries I went to try to get from the mouths of the fishermen who had taken part in the rescue at the time and were still in good health as much as possible of the original history that would not be blown away by this typhoon.

From Shenjiamen the ferry took four hours. I first came directly to Qingbang Island, an administrative district under the control of Dongji Town in Putuo District. Because of sea sickness, I nearly missed the island. Fortunately the kind captain turned around and called out to a Qingbang fisherman's boat to carry me ashore. When I asked the fisherman about the way to Shen Agui's house, he said, "Another one come to interview him! OK, take the mountain road, follow the road all the way down to a village. There's a strong wind; take care." The young fisherman spoke quite smooth Mandarin.

After walking for forty minutes, with directions from no less than four fishermen, I reached Shen Agui's home. Only he and his wife lived in the two storey brick and tiled house. The family moved in here in 1962. Shen Agui is eighty-two this year, and as a boat captain for more than sixty years he was still going strong. When this elderly man spoke of the past he often jumped up and down with enthusiasm and had a remarkable voice and expression. Because of issues with the language dialect, several times he stopped and wrote down what he was saying word by word for me.

"Basically our whole village went to rescue people. That year I was only nineteen. I had never seen foreigners and did not understand their language. At that time I didn't give it much thought, but just got in the boat and went to rescue people. Rescuing people is important; after all you can't just helplessly watch them being washed away by the waves, eh." Shen Agui explained that at the time thirty boats went out. The British men were mostly more than 1.7 metres tall; their clothes were in tatters, some were wearing only shorts, desperately struggling in the sea. "The boat that dad, uncle and I went in to rescue people had a hole and water was seeping in, so we had to bail out on one side and rescue people on the other side. We rescued seven British men."

After the rescue, the island increased by so many people that it was necessary for everyone to take the British soldiers into their homes, the temple, and in the alleys. The original temple in which the British soldiers were placed has now become a local old people's activity centre.

The elderly Shen Agui withstood the strong sunshine and took me to Chen Yonghua's home in the second village. Because of the physical features of Qingbang, it is naturally divided into the first, second, third and fourth villages. Chen Yonghua is seventy-eight years old. That year at the age of only fifteen he witnessed and took part in the entire process of the rescue. He pointed at the sea and said to me, at that time Qingbang only had thatched cottages; there were no brick and tiled houses. Everyone was very poor, the cottages were very low. "Look at the shore by the pier, you can clearly see the sea conditions." He and old Shen Agui accompanied me to the place on the coast where the British prisoners of war had been rescued and brought ashore that year. The two elderly men looked at the ocean and suddenly fell silent.

At present in Qingbang there is an elderly grandmother in good health called Wang Jiaoyun, eighty-eight years old. She is the wife of one of those who launched the rescue that year, Tang Ruliang. Regarding the past, she waves her hands. I don't know if her memory is gradually getting dimmer, or if she doesn't want to say any more, just, "That year everyone from the village saved people: that's as it should be, it's the proper thing to do." The picture she remembered most deeply was putting hot baked sweet potatoes into the hands of the British men who had fallen victim. The British people were not used to the smell and taste of fresh fish and seafood, and sweet potato was the best staple diet of the whole village. The elderly grandmother was hard of hearing, but liked to smoke. The old villager next to me told me that round about the time of liberation[108] her husband had gone from Hong Kong to Taiwan and had not come back again.

Returning from Qingbang, I took the fishing boat used by the Qingbang villagers, so as to avoid the typhoon. Shen Agui insisted on seeing me onto the boat. Ahead of the typhoon, the waves tossed the boat up and down. A ray of sunlight came down. I sat in a fishing boat for the first time in my life and saw a few Chinese characters, "Stand steady in wind and waves". Watching the bronzed back of the operator of the diesel engined boat was like seeing again a figure of the former generation who rowed out to rescue people that year.

After the boat had been going for about twenty minutes, I reached the location of the Dongji Town government, Miaozihu. Nowadays this has gradually developed locally into a tourist destination. Apparently Li Qingzhao[109] made a spiritual tour of this place and wrote her famous work, *Proud fishing family*.

The fishermen from here rescued one hundred and six British prisoners of war from the *Lisbon Maru*. Lin Furong[110] and Wu Lanfang are the only two old men still around and in good health who took part in the rescue at the time.

When I tried to find the elderly Lin Fuyun, he had just gone to his neighbours house to play mah-jong. "Old Lin is fine, his eyes and ears are also working well." His wife greeted me warmly. However hard I tried, I did not completely hear her name clearly. I only know that she is six years younger than Lin Fuyun. This year she is seventy-five. Looking at her, she is a kindly and honest fishing family wife. She nimbly called her husband back. As soon as he saw me, Lin Fuyun stepped over very quickly. After years of fishing, up to now he is still proud that in that year he rescued sixteen people from the sea.

Secrets of the sinking of the *Lisbon Maru* incident unveiled
Zhejiang Daily: Reporters Zhang Xueqin and Shen Guan[111]

An historical file called L030-236 made up fifty-seven years ago is kept in the Special Collections Room of the Zhejiang Province Archives. On opening the front cover of this file, one's eyes light on the first document, which is a telex written entirely in English.

This was from the then (12 April 1948) British Ambassador to China to the Chinese Foreign Ministry. The thrust of the telex was as follows.

During the Second World War, a Japanese ship, the *Lisbon Maru*, transported nearly two thousand British prisoners of war from Hong Kong towards Japan. On 2 October 1942, whilst the ship was sailing in the seas off Zhoushan, it was attacked by torpedos and sank. At the time, more than two hundred British prisoners of war were saved from drowning by the courageous efforts of the fishermen of East Fisherman Island,[112] Zhoushan, to rescue them. Despite the fishermen's livelihoods being very poor, they did everything they could to provide those British prisoners of war with food, shelter and care, enabling them to survive.

On 3 October, the Japanese soldiers sent gunboats to surround the island and took away the British prisoners of war. Later, the local Chinese fishermen also risked their lives to protect three of the British prisoners of war and finally sent them safely to Allied jurisdiction.

In order to thank the Chinese Zhoushan fishermen for their dauntless spirit in carrying out the rescue, the British government has assigned a special fund as a reward, to be presented to the local fishermen. At the same time, the Royal Navy plans to send a destroyer HMS *McCaw*[113] to go to East Fisherman Island in Zhoushan to hold a presentation ceremony.

The second document was dated 16 April 1948. It was an express letter written from the then Chinese Ministry of Foreign Affairs to the Zhejiang Provincial Government. The letter required Zhejiang Province to check and verify "whether or not" the fishermen from East Fisherman Island in Zhoushan "indeed rescued endangered British prisoners of war on the *Lisbon Maru* on 2 October 1942."

The final document in the file is a paper submitted by Dongji Township in Zhoushan with details of the process of the rescue of the British prisoners of war. The main contents are as follows:

East Fish Father Island, which should be named East Fisherman Island, is an historic place name and is now called Qingbang Island. In the early morning of 2 October 1942, local fishermen heard a thunderous noise from out in the ocean. Later people in trouble appeared struggling in the ocean. As suggested by Tang Ruliang's group of five men,[114] all the fishermen on the island paddled their boats out to take part in the rescue, saving altogether 216 people. Neighbouring Miaozihu Island also launched a rescue, initiated by Shen Wanshou's group of five,[115] and altogether saved 106 people. Another small island, Xifushan Island, also rescued sixty-two people. Some of those rescued showed the five Chinese characters for Hong Kong British (香港英國人) and only then did the fishermen know that they were allied prisoners of war who had fallen into the clutches of the Japanese army.

Seeing these prisoners of war suffering from hunger and cold, the fishermen from these small islands one after another gave them clothes, food and shelter. A few persuasive fishermen on Qingbang Island then began to discuss how the allied prisoners of war could be safely transferred. But there was no prospect of a positive outcome to the discussions. On the morning of 3 October, five Japanese gunboats appeared, surrounding these islands. Tang Ruliang and the others on Qingbang Island hastily hid the three men who appeared to be the leaders of the British prisoners in a cave on the island. That afternoon, two hundred fully armed Japanese soldiers carried out a house-to-house search for the British prisoners. The result was that apart from the three men in the cave, the remaining 381 British prisoners of war were all taken away by the Japanese army. For several days afterwards, enemy ships continually patrolled around these islands.

On 9 October, there were no more enemy ships patrolling around Qingbang Island. Fisherman Tang Pin'gen and six others took the risk of using a small sailing boat to get the three British prisoners of war to Hulu Island, and handed them over to the department of Wang Jineng of the 4th Regiment of the Japanese resistance at that time. Later they passed through many places and were sent to Chongqing.

After victory in the War of Resistance against Japan the three British people who had been saved made contact with Tang Ruliang and Wang Jineng. The British Embassy, possibly after an introduction from these three British people, only knew that Qingbang Island had rescued more than 200 British prisoners of war. In fact, adding on Miaozihu and the others 384 British POWs were rescued.

The "Process of the Rescue" had an attachment with a register of names, all were the names of the fishermen who had rescued British prisoners of war that year. With a rescue on such a scale, why had Dongji Township never reported this upwards? In fact, after the victory in the War of Resistance the township intended to report upwards, but the simple answer was, "We don't want to take credit for others' achievements." Therefore, this time the township again requested the fishermen who had taken part in the rescue that year to register their names, when accepting the grant. The fishermen were still not willing to register. Finally, only after the township did a lot of explanatory work and registration work were they able to open the register. But Shen Wanshou, who had launched the rescue of the British POWs said very clearly he would "not accept a grant".

Although the historical documents on the rescuing of British prisoners of war from the *Lisbon Maru* have never been publicly revealed, in the age of reform and opening up[116] there have always been people from civil society taking an interest in this affair. Retired veteran cadre Mao Dechuan started investigating this incident. Later, Zhang Jian and Guan Yixing of the Cultural Department, Wang Yongjian of the original Zhoushan Marine Fisheries Company and others, have all been to Qingbang Island, Miaozihu Island and Xifushan Island (currently all under the administration of Dongji Island) to conduct on-the-spot investigations, and accumulated much valuable historical material from oral accounts.

When the Zhoushan fishermen saw the Westerners on the *Lisbon Maru* on the verge of death, the traditional moral virtue of saving lives immediately urged them to use every effort to go and rescue people. Later, when they learned that these Westerners were allied prisoners of war, these poor fishermen then went out of their way to provide them with clothing, food and shelter.

People's exhibits

Fisherman Zhang Fuqing's boat went out to sea to rescue people. The little boat was already full of British prisoners of war, but Zhang Fuqing heard music coming from rocks to the side and rowed his boat over to the rocks. There were three British prisoners of war on the rocks, one of whom was playing a mouth organ. The intention was clear: he hoped someone would rescue him. Later, this British prisoner who was playing the mouth organ went into the sea, hung over the side of Zhang Fuqing's boat and swam to Qingbang Island. To thank him for his kindness in saving his life, this British prisoner gave the mouth organ to Zhang Fuqing as a present. So, many fishermen on Qingbang Island knew Zhang Fuqing had a special mouth organ. But, not long afterwards, because in fact life was too hard, in the end Zhang Fuqing's wife took the mouth organ to Shanghai and exchanged it for one hectolitre of rice. Wang Yongjian said, "Today, when Zhang Fuqing's son Zhang Dingkang talks about this, he still feels great regret. If the mouth organ was still around, this would surely be a precious piece of historical evidence."

In fact, there are still fishermen locally who are keeping things given to them as presents that year by British prisoners of war. Fisherman Ren Furen of Qingbang Island also took part in the rescue activities. Later, a rescued British POW gave him a western cook's knife. Wang Yongjian said, "Nowadays, this western cook's knife is being kept by his daughter Ren Meijun as a keepsake."

People's investigations have unearthed a crucial figure. In the final analysis, the reason why three British prisoners of war were able to escape successfully depended on the wartime-appointed Deputy Commander of the 4th Regiment, Miao Kaiyun. Such a crucial figure, why can his name not be seen in the historical documents? The written memories of those involved have solved the mystery.

The person who wrote the written memories is named as Wang Jineng in the historical documents. In the articles he wrote whilst still alive, were details of the process by which Miao Kaiyun helped three British prisoners of war to escape.

At that time, Miao Kaiyun was on Hulu Island as a guest in his father-in-law's house. On hearing that there were allied prisoners of war on Qingbang Island, he ran the risk of taking a boat to go there. On Qingbang Island, after he had spoken to the three prisoners of war, he immediately arranged people and a boat to transfer them, from Qingbang to Guoju, then to Kangtou, afterward to Xiangshan; and he sent soldiers to guard them all the way. Finally, the three prisoners of war went to Yunhe and after passing through many places they reached Chongqing. Wang Jineng's account said, "Miao Kaiyun's contribution in the rescue of three British prisoners of war really cannot go unrecognised."

But in the period of the 1948 civil war between the Chinese Nationalist Party and the Chinese Communist Party Miao Kaiyun was killed by local officials on a fabricated charge.

No wonder that in the historical documents there is only the name of the Regimental Commander, Wang Jineng, but not the name of the Deputy Commander, Miao Kaiyun.

In Zhoushan the author saw an historic photograph. The figures in the photograph included Wang Jineng and Miao Kaiyun, and with them were the three rescued British prisoners of war, who were all wearing Chinese style fishermen's clothes that had been provided. This is also a valuable piece of historic visual evidence!

An even greater piece of historical evidence should be a motorised boat. Wang Yongjian said that in the end, the British naval ship did not come to Dongji Island to present funds. We have gleaned from looking through old newspapers, that on 18 February 1949, the British held a thanksgiving ceremony. The then Governor of Hong Kong, Sir Alexander Grantham, on behalf of the British government presented a motorised fishing boat, *Sea Peace*, as a gift to Dongji Township in Zhoushan. However, at present , there is no one who can say clearly what finally happened to it.

Overseas historical material

Today there are twenty fortunate survivors who were prisoners of war on the *Lisbon Maru* that year. British scholar Tony Banham, who researches the sinking of the *Lisbon Maru* Incident, keeps in constant contact with these survivors. From these survivors, Tony has learned the true facts and of the kindness of the Chinese people. This scholar was invited to arrive in Zhoushan on 2 April to meet Chinese researchers and fishermen who rescued British prisoners of war that year.

After contacting Tony, a complete picture of the sinking of the *Lisbon Maru* Incident starts to unfold before one's eyes. The prisoners of war on the *Lisbon Maru* altogether numbered 1,816.[117] All were British officers and soldiers who had fought the Japanese in Hong Kong that year (and including some officers' families).[118] The *Lisbon Maru* was a refitted cargo ship with three cargo holds below deck, divided into forward, midships and aft. The Japanese army put the prisoners of war into these three holds. Because the holds were small and there were a lot of people, everyone could only stand. The three holds became simply three tin cans filled with people. On the deck were more than 770 fully armed Japanese soldiers.

At the time, the Japanese army wanted to take these prisoners of war from Hong Kong to Japanese soil. But the Japanese army had put no sign on the *Lisbon Maru* that she was a prisoner of war ship. In the early morning of 1 October 1942, after the submarine SS-214/USS *Grouper* patrolling in the high seas off Zhoushan had discovered the ship, she fired torpedos at her, one of which hit the ship. But the *Lisbon Maru* did not sink immediately.

That afternoon, Japanese destroyers and transport ships went to the area of the incident and most of the Japanese soldiers who were on board the *Lisbon Maru* were transferred to these ships. However, at this crucial moment, the Japanese soldiers went so far as to completely secure the hatches. The officers amongst the British prisoners of war protested, requesting that one plank be removed from each of the holds to allow the prisoners to get some fresh air. But not only did this request meet with refusal from the Japanese army, Japanese soldiers even covered the hatches with tarpaulin thereby making the air in the holds even more foul.

On the morning of 2 October, twenty-four hours after the torpedo attack, the ship had still not sunk and had drifted to three miles from Qingbang Island. But the after-hold was already letting in water. In extremely foul air, the prisoners in the after-hold took turns in using a foot pump to bail out the water.

After 8.00am, the remaining Japanese soldiers and ship's crew began to evacuate the ship. The prisoners in the holds started to save themselves. Those in the forward and midships holds eventually with difficulty opened the hatches and climbed onto the deck. The Japanese soldiers opened fire on them. Before long, the ship's stern sank further into the water. The prisoners in the after- hold were not able to open the hatch, and all perished.[119]

The prisoners who rushed out of the holds jumped into the sea one after another and swam towards the islands. Many of them drowned at sea.

One survivor recalled later, "A miracle happened! A Chinese fishing fleet came and started to rescue us. I was one of those rescued. All those rescued were very lucky, including me. After we were rescued we stayed in a place called Qingbang".

"These Chinese people treated the prisoners of war with great kindness, giving us food and the Chinese people's own clothes."

In his reminiscences, survivor Col Hamilton[120] had this to say, "The original idea of the Japanese was to let all the prisoners of war drown. That way they could say the ship had been sunk by the Americans and they had had no opportunity to carry out a rescue. Later, once the Japanese army saw that the Chinese had rescued so many prisoners of war, they realised they could not carry out their plan and changed their policy."

Originally, the prisoners of war on the *Lisbon Maru* could all have been saved, the Japanese army could have transferred them to other ships together with their own soldiers, but did not do so.

Thus, in the high seas off Dongji Island, Zhoushan, not only was there a big ship sunk, but also left are the remains of nearly 1,000 British Army officers and soldiers (currently the most conservative estimate is that at the time more than 840[121] died).

History is a looking-glass: only by looking over history and reflecting on history can we look into the future. This is also where the significance of the concern of the Chinese civil population for this affair and the British scholar's research into this affair lies.

Special thanks are expressed for the great support of the Zhejiang Provincial Archives and the Zhoushan City Archives in the writing of this article.

Appendices

Timeline of the *Lisbon Maru* incident[122]

31 May 1920	Launch of The *Lisbon Maru* built in Yokohama.
27 October 1941	USS *Grouper* launched in Connecticut.
8 December 1941	Japan launches the Pacific War, Japan invades Hong Kong, battle breaks out with the defending forces.
8 December 1941[123]	Japanese troops land on Hong Kong Island, defending troops move to the south of the island for defence.
25 December 1941	Hong Kong defending troops announce a surrender after 18 days of fighting.
Late January 1942	The Japanese army sends all former Hong Kong government officials, businessmen and their families, altogether about 3,000 people, to Stanley Internment Camp.
Late January 1942	Because of excessive overcrowding in Shamshuipo Camp, about 2,000 prisoners of war are transferred to North Point Camp.
20 February 1942	The Japanese Army announces that Hong Kong is Japanese occupied territory.
April 1942	The Japanese Army officially designates Shamshuipo Camp as only for the imprisonment of other ranks. All officers are moved to Argyle Street Concentration Camp.
June 1942	The *Lisbon Maru* undergoes maintenance at Taikoo Dockyard.
28 August 1942	USS *Grouper* of the 81st Division of the US Pacific Fleet leaves Pearl Harbour to carry out maritime patrol duties.
1 September 1942	USS *Grouper* reaches the waters around Midway Island.
25 September 1942	The Japanese Army assembles 1,816 [124] British prisoners of war in Shamshuipo prisoner of war camp and announces they will be sent to Japan for their sicknesses to be cured.
27 September 1942	The Japanese freighter the *Lisbon Maru*, carrying 1,816 [125] British prisoners of war sets sail for Japan.

30 September 1942	The *Lisbon Maru* passes the Beiyushan lighthouse, encounters a storm, and sails out of coastal waters.
4.00am 1 October 1942	USS *Grouper* sees traces of the *Lisbon Maru* in the moonlight.
7.04am on 1 October 1942	USS *Grouper* fires three torpedos at the *Lisbon Maru* from a range of 3,200 metres.
7.15am on 1 October 1942	The fourth torpedo fires and hits the propeller at the stern.
8.45am on 1 October 1942	USS *Grouper* fires the fifth torpedo at the *Lisbon Maru* at a range of 1,000 metres.
9.37am on 1 October 1942	USS *Grouper* fires the sixth torpedo at the *Lisbon Maru*.
Midday on 1 October 1942	Water enters No. 3 Hold on the *Lisbon Maru*, prisoners of war frantically bail out the water with a foot pump.
Afternoon of 1 October 1942	Japanese navy destroyer *Kuroshio Maru* arrives in neighbouring waters.
5.00pm on 1 October 1942	More than 700 Japanese officers and soldiers start to transfer from the *Lisbon Maru* to the *Kuroshio Maru*.
Sunrise on 2 October 1942	The hull of the *Lisbon Maru* shakes. A small group of prisoners of war starts to try to open the hatches.
8.10am on 2 October 1942	The captain decides to abandon ship and transfers to another Japanese warship (*Toyokuni Maru*) with the remaining Japanese troops.
About 9.00am on 2 October 1942	First successful break-out by the prisoners of war; shot at by Japanese soldiers.
About 9.00am on 2 October 1942	All Japanese troops leave the *Lisbon Maru*; prisoners of war hurriedly flee from the holds.
10.00am on 2 October 1942	The *Lisbon Maru* sinks; the Royal Artillery unit in No. 3 Hold are unfortunately stranded in the hold, all soldiers go down with the ship.[126]
2 October 1942	Fishermen from Dongji Island rescue 384 British prisoners of war.
3 October 1942	Several Japanese bombers fly over Dongji Island airspace and drop many bombs.
4 October 1942	Five Japanese warships surround Dongji Island.

5 October 1942	Japanese warships transport 381 captured British prisoners of war to Shanghai.
9 October 1942	Miao Kaiyun and others start to transport the three prisoners who had been hiding in Child Cave to Hulu Island by sampan.
10 October 1942	The *Shinsei Maru*, carrying prisoners of war, arrives at the port of Moji; the prisoners of war are transferred to camps all over Japan.
10 October 1942	The three prisoners continue to be secretly transported to inland China.
1 June 1945	Osaka prisoner of war camp raised to the ground in a fierce bombing raid by a US B29 bomber.
15 August 1945	Japan formally announces unconditional surrender.
17 February 1949	The Hong Kong Governor, Sir Alexander Grantham, on behalf of the British Government, presents a motorised fishing boat to the Dongji Island fishermen.

Map of the track of the *Lisbon Maru* and the areas passed[127]

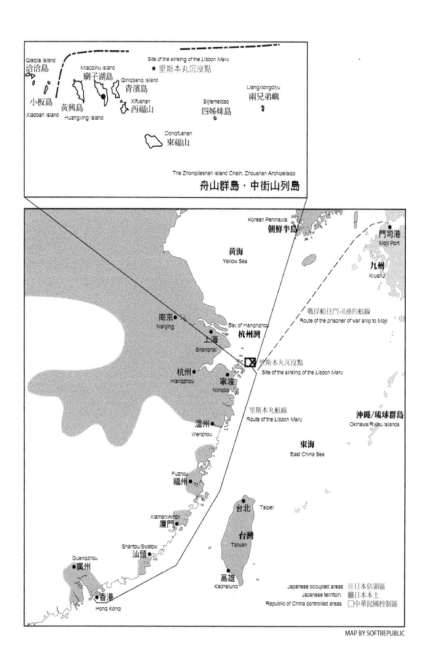

Description of USS *Grouper*[128]

The USS *Grouper* was the third conventionally-powered Gato Class submarine in the US Navy. The keel was laid down and construction started in December 1940 in Groton, Connecticut, by the Electric Boat Company, and it was launched in October 1941. It was taken into active service the next year at the nearby US Navy's New London Naval Base. The first captain was LCDR CE Duke, and after being taken into active service the *Grouper* went to join the Pacific Submarine Fleet located in the Pearl Harbour Naval Base in Hawaii in the Pacific Ocean.

In the Battle of Midway at the beginning of June 1942, the USS *Grouper* did not directly engage in combat. Although whilst cruising it discovered a Japanese aircraft carrier that had suffered heavy losses from the US forces, lacking other support it did not mount an attack.

At that time, because battery storage technology had just begun, the submerged depth of a submarine was shallow, and the submerged speed was extremely low (the planned submerged speed of the *Grouper* was only two knots). During the Second World War, submarines from all nations normally cruised on the surface like ordinary ships. Furthermore, the open style diesel engine, whilst burning oxygen from the air, drives the electric generator fully charging the batteries. [129] This means the submarine can only dive when in action and avoiding gunfire, so on the submarine, apart from ten torpedo tubes, there are also weapons that don't exist on modern submarines – anti-aircraft and surface cannon and machine-guns.

Also, the main weapon of the submarine – torpedos, the same as other torpedos at that time, used inertial navigation – and was just fired in a straight line, but in view of the design failure of the Mark 14 the submerged depth was insufficient, and it could easily be discovered with the naked eye by lookouts on the target which could turn to avoid it, so it was often necessary to fire many torpedos to hit the target (which is why the USS *Grouper* fired as many as six torpedos to hit the cargo ship the *Lisbon Maru*).

After the Battle of Midway Island in which Japanese forces suffered heavy losses, power in the North Pacific tilted towards the USA. US forces began to launch a campaign to control Japanese waters by attacking Japanese merchant shipping with the submarine fleet. The *Grouper* was one of the submarines mobilised.

USS *Grouper* SS-214

Displacement (surfaced)	1,870 tons
Displacement (submerged)	2,424 tons
Overall length	311.75 feet
Height of vessel	27.25 feet
Breadth of vessel	19.25 feet
Propulsion	4 diesel engines; 2 electric propellers; 2 X 126 storage batteries
Power	5400 Horsepower 4026.78 Kilowatts.
Propellers	2
Speed	Surface: 20.25 knots; submerged: 8.75 knots
Range and endurance	11,000 miles (at 10 knots); 48 hours (underwater at 2 knots)
Submerged depth	300 feet
Armament	8^{130}X 21 inch torpedo tubes (6 forward, 4 aft); 24 Mark 14 Torpedos.

On 12 June after receiving supplies from the Midway Island Naval Base, USS *Grouper* started for the Western Pacific Ocean – the Japanese controlled East China Sea area – and set off to

carry out its first war patrol, launching surprise attacks on all enemy ships flying the rising sun flag of Japanese imperialism.

After damaging two Japanese merchant vessels in the East China Sea, the *Grouper* returned to Pearl Harbour for repairs and resupply on 30 July. Its second combat patrol began only on 28 August. During the second combat patrol on its return to the waters of the East China Sea, after the *Grouper* successfully sank the Japanese merchant ships *Tone Maru* and the *Lisbon Maru*, it returned to base, although only in the aftermath did they learn that the latter ship was a prisoner-of-war ship fully loaded with allied prisoners of war.

During the third combat patrol the *Grouper* added further to its combat successes by sinking the Japanese merchant ship *Bandoeng Maru* which was loaded with supplies for the Japanese forces on the Solomon Islands.

The third combat patrol in November and December was conducted in the south, in the seas off Brisbane, Australia.

The *Grouper*'s final combat success was in December 1944, when it sank the comandeered merchant ship the *Kumanoyama Maru*, sailing under the Mitsui OSK Line flag.

After the War was over the *Grouper* did not retire from naval service; in 1946 it underwent a major refit, and was in service throughout the US-Soviet cold war, formally retiring from service only in 1968, and in 1970 was sold to a factory owner for scrap.

The *Lisbon Maru*
Another Japanese freighter buried in the Pacific Ocean[131]

The *Lisbon Maru* was a passenger-cargo merchant ship of the Japanese NYK Line, with a length of approximately 120 metres, a beam of about eighteen metres, a mast about twenty meters high and a displacement of 7,152 tons. Construction of the keel of the *Lisbon Maru* began on 15 October 1919 with hull number 70. Construction was carried out by the Yokohama Dock Company Limited. She had two sister ships, the *Lyons Maru* and the *Lima Maru*.

On 5 May 1934 she sailed to San Francisco Harbour carrying a group of Japanese migrants, and the following year a photograph was taken of her in the Thames Estuary, near London. Between June and the end of August 1942 British secret agents traced the *Lisbon Maru* to Taikoo Dock in Hong Kong undergoing maintenance. According to British intelligence officials in Chongqing at that time, the *Lisbon Maru* had possibly been damaged by a mine or a torpedo.

During this period, all Japanese merchant ships had been commandeered by the military to transport strategic goods and materials, even troops and equipment, and immediately after the maintenance and refitting of the *Lisbon Maru* had been completed, she became a troop transporter, transporting troops to the battlefield in Guadalcanal in the South Pacific to resist the Allied counteroffensive led by US forces. After the *Lisbon Maru* had completed her task, she again returned to Hong Kong, to prepare to take prisoners of war imprisoned in Shamshuipo concentration camp to Japan.

In 1942, the *Lisbon Maru* entered her 22nd year, which was her last. The captain appointed was Kiyoda Shigeru, who had graduated from Marine School in December 1921 and served on a number of merchant ships. In 4 March 1942 the ship he was in charge of, the *Morioka Maru*, was sunk by a mine in Nagasaki. Afterwards he was posted to the *Calcutta Maru*, which was sunk by a torpedo from the American submarine USS *Triton* soon afterwards.

Lisbon Maru

(NYK Museum)

Length	120 metres
Beam	18 metres
Height of mast	20 metres
Displacement	7,152 tons
Launched	31 May 1920
Builders	Yokohama Dock Company

The US forces at that time adopted a submarine strategy to deal with the Japanese marine supply line. Starting in 1942 they sank thousands of Japanese merchant ships, leading directly to completely cutting off the Japanese overseas supply line, causing a situation of serious shortages of raw materials and goods and equipment for its munitions factories and all kinds of military equipment; and there was no way to transport oil to Japan, one of the most important fuels for driving the war machine.

Kiyoda Shigeru, after having twice had a ship in his charge sunk within two months, on 9 September in the same year was appointed as captain of the *Lisbon Maru*, and he boarded the ship and assumed his appointment on 15 September. The ship was first loaded with 1,676 tons of copper, scrap iron, cotton, lead, cloth and all kinds of ore in preparation for shipment to Osaka, as well as thirty-two tons of high performance 5-inch artillery shells to be transported to Tokyo. Apart from these strategic materials, Kiyoda Shigeru would soon see nearly two thousand British prisoners of war and more than seven hundred Japanese troops board the ship.

With its name painted on the bow in white in English and Japanese, and flying the flag of the Rising Sun, the *Lisbon Maru* prepared to set out on its dangerous journey to return to Japan. At this time Kiyoda Shigeru's heart must have been pounding: worrying whether this more than seven thousand tons *Lisbon Maru*, very much bigger than the other ships he had captained previously, would be able to escape the misfortune of being sunk by an American naval submarine.

List of residents of Dongji Island, Dinghai County who rescued British prisoners of war[132]

Hu Afa
Li Chaoxiang
Guo Haibao
Huang Kangxin
Tang Ruliang
Tang Shunyu
Shi Xiandiao
Shen Guixing
Li Chaohong
Liu Arong
Zhuang Axin
Zhou Zhangfu
Tang Caigen
Liu Quanming
Tong Laisheng
Li Changgen
Yan Azhao
Wang Ruiyuan
Chen Aqing
Liu Kaiming
Hou Ahou
Wang Danying
Chen Xinghua
Zhang Aliang
Chen Xinding
Fang Aquan
Chen Apin
Dou Rugen
Zhang Afu
Chen Xingfu
Chen Xinliang
Bian Derong
Qiu Awei
Zhang Fuqing
Chen Rusheng
Chen Xinyue

Guo Ade
Zhang Chunshui
Guo Fuqing
Shi Alin
Dou Akang
Huang Jinfu
Hu Azhi
Li Chaoneng
Guo Haifu
Huang Hanlin
Wang Bangrong
Huang Anfu
Shi Sanmei
Shen Tingui
Li Chaoliang
Liu Zhuhong
Wu Alu
Tang Chongqing
Shi Xianjun
Chen Apin
Li Caixing
Du Agen
Shu Zhipin
Chong Xinquan
Lin Shengtian
Shen Agui
Wei Anxin
Tang Abao
Chen Akang
Zhang Zongliang
Chen Yazi
Liu Aren
Chen Songgen
Wang Renyou
Zhang Apin
Zhang Songfa

Guo Xinfa
Li Hulu
Ye Ruigen
Zhuang Abao
Dou Rufu
Ren Xinjian
Liu Ade
Yuan Zhongde
Tan Atai
Shi Xiantong
Zhu Ade
Ren Congjin
Li Chaoyue
Ye Ziyu
Guo Fubao
Yan Apin
Dou Ruisheng
Huang Ahai
Hu Kechuan
Li Aqing
Li Rufu
Chen Zhongyue
Liu Yongxing
Chen Songmao
Bian Dingxing
Zhang Asan
Zhang Yongqing
Chen Songying
Chen Genhua
Chong Ahua
Liu Akang
Shen Yousheng
Hou Agen
Zhang Rupin
Chen Minghai
Chen Shunpin

Wang Arong
Li Xiaolian
Dou Rukang
Weng Songdi
Yan Hexiang
Wei Fuchang
Wu Yeniao
Liu Dunfang
Wu Yunyuan
Hu Xiaoniao
Zhao Azhang
Yan Heming
Han Yeyuan
Wang Youbang
Chen Yinren
Huang Caigeng
Lin Xinfa
Chen Ayu
Hu Daniao
Huang Xingzhao
Gan Yefa
Ma Xinzi
Zhou Jikun
Zhao Xianqi
Wei Ruitang
Lü Deren
Xu Wenrui
Weng Yifang

Chen Amao
Guo Afu
Zhang Changfa
Shen Fuming
Wang Dayun
Huang Yeming
Wu Qisan
Wu Lanfang
Wu Shangshui
Liang Agou
Chen Linke
Wu Haopan
Wei Fulai
Wang Xianlin
Wang Yehai
Wu Yunhe
Wu Qilin
Weng Jiuxing
Yan Heyun
Huang Ruilong
Wei Yegou
Wang Yebiao
Wu Yecun
Lin Yehuai
Zhang Yemou
Lin Meilan
Wu Qisheng
Lin Dingzhang

Liu Afu
Tang Aliang
Zhao Xiaoru
Xu Yede
Dou Yede
Lin Fuyin
Wang Yeji
Huang Ruixian
Zhao Xianlin
Liang Afa
Shen Baoxing
Wang Xiaoyun
Huang Mingde
Wang Yefu
Wu Yunlong
Wu Shangheng
Cai Jieshou
Weng Arong
Lin Yefa
Huang Ruiyuan
Wang Yeming
Chen Yeyou
Wu Shangde
Fang Laiyun
Ma Caiming
Ren Linsheng
Wang Shiyi
ShenYuanxing

List of victims of the *Lisbon Maru*
Reproduced by kind permission of Tony Banham[133]

Name	Regt or Corps	Unit
ABEL Clifford Alan	RN	HMS *Tamar*
ADAM George Currie	The Royal Scots	2nd Bn
ADAMS William	RA	15 AA Bty 8 Coast Regt
ADAMSON Charles Vincent	HKSRA	1st Bty
AIKMAN Ronald Edward	The Middlesex Regt	1st Bn
ALCHIN Milton Carl	Dockyard Defence Corps	Dockyard Police
ALEXANDER Adam Glen	RA	12th Coast Bty
ALLAN Hugh Hamilton	The Royal Scots	2nd Bn
ALLANSON Kenneth Edward	RA	15 AA Bty 8 Coast Regt
ALLEN William Richard	Royal Marines	HMS *Tamar*
ALLIN Bernard Lester	Royal Signal Corps	HK Signal Coy
ALLISON Patrick Joseph	The Royal Scots	2nd Bn
ALLPORT Albert Edward	HKSRA	1st Bty
AMBROSE Fred	Royal Marines	HMS *Tamar*
ANDERSON John	RA	12th Coast Bty
ANDERSON John McLeod	The Royal Scots	2nd Bn
ANDREW Matthew Beaton	The Royal Scots	2nd Bn
ANDREWS Leslie William	The Middlesex Regt	1st Bn
ARCHER Albert William	RN	HMS *Thracian*
ARCHIBALD Robert Miller	The Royal Scots	2nd Bn
ARCHIBALD William	The Royal Scots	2nd Bn
ARNDLE Edward	RA	12th Coast Bty
ASHFORD Ronald Edward	RN	HMS *Tamar*
ASTILL Arthur	RA	15 AA Bty 8 Coast Regt
ATKINSON Edwin	Royal Signal Corps	HK Signal Coy
ATKINSON Robert	RN	HMS *Tamar*
ATTWELL Gerald	RN	HMS *Tamar*
AUDSLEY Harold	RE	40 Fortress Coy
AULD Alexander	The Royal Scots	2nd Bn

AUSTIN William	HKSRA	1st Bty
BACHE Herbert Henry	RAMC	27 Coy
BACKHURST Alfred Leonard	The Middlesex Regt	1st Bn
BADER Bernard John	HKSRA	1st Bty
BAILEY Albert William Henry	RA	8 Coast Regt
BAILEY Reginald Kenneth	RN	HMS *Tamar*
BAIN John Harper	The Royal Scots	2nd Bn
BAKER George Sidney	The Middlesex Regt	1st Bn
BAKER Jack	RN	HMS *Tamar*
BAKER John James	The Middlesex Regt	1st Bn
BALAAM Arthur John	RA	15 AA Bty 8 Coast Regt
BALDWIN William Charles	RA	12th Coast Bty
BANKS Raymond	RA	15 AA Bty 8 Coast Regt
BARBOUR James Munro	RE	40 Fortress Coy
BARLOW William Arthur	RA	12th Coast Bty
BARNES Cyril	RA	7 Bty 5 HAA Regt
BARNES John	The Royal Scots	2nd Bn
BARNES John[134]	RA	15 AA Bty 8 Coast Regt
BARNES Walter	The Middlesex Regt	1st Bn
BARRATT Walter Arthur	The Middlesex Regt	1st Bn
BARRETT John Charles	The Middlesex Regt	1st Bn
BASKERVILLE Albert Thomas	RA	12th Coast Bty
BATES Ronald Langley	RE	40 Fortress Coy
BATH Ronald Jack	The Middlesex Regt	1st Bn
BAXTER James Philip	RA	24 Heavy Bty
BEATON James Thom	RA	12th Coast Bty
BEDFORD George	Royal Signal Corps	HK Signal Coy
BEESLEY Norman	RE	22 Fortress Coy
BELL David Bowie	The Royal Scots	2nd Bn
BENNETT John	The Middlesex Regt	1st Bn
BENNETT Leonard Charles	The Middlesex Regt	1st Bn
BENNISON William	RA	15 AA Bty 8 Coast Regt
BENSON Joseph Hugh	RN	HMS *Tamar*

155

BERRY Ralph	RA	15 AA Bty 8 Coast Regt
BERRY Thomas Malcolm	The Royal Scots	2nd Bn
BEST Harold Ernest	RN	HMS *Tamar*
BEVIS Herbert Thomas	RN	HMS *Tamar*
BICKMORE Ernest Alfred	RN	HMS *Tamar*
BIGGS Arthur Leonard	RN	RNVR
BILTON Arthur	RN	HMS *Tamar*
BIRCH Arthur Edward	RN	HMS *Tamar*
BLACK Andrew Christie	The Royal Scots	2nd Bn
BLACK George	RA	12th Coast Bty
BLACKMAN Albert Lionel	RE	22 Fortress Coy
BLISS David Ken	RN	HMS *Tamar*
BOAG John Law	RE	40 Fortress Coy
BOND James William	The Middlesex Regt	1st Bn
BOND William Horace	RN	HMS *Tamar*
BONFIELD Frank	RN	HMS *Tamar*
BOOTHROYD George H	RN	HMS *Tamar*
BOWDITCH Alfred Edward	RA	8 Coast Regt
BOWEY George Henry	The Middlesex Regt	1st Bn
BOYCE Samuel John	RA	965 Defence Bty
BOYES William James L	RN	HMS *Tamar*
BOYLE Hugh	The Royal Scots	2nd Bn
BOYLE Thomas John	RA	12th Coast Bty
BOYNE Martin William A	RN	HMS *Tamar*
BRADFORD Alfred Thomas	The Middlesex Regt	1st Bn
BREMNER William	RA	8 Coast Regt
BRENNAN Michael	RE	22 Fortress Coy
BRIGHT Arthur William	RN	HMS *Tamar*
BROCKLEY Wilfred	RAMC	Attached unit
BROOKS Charles Frederick	RA	12th Coast Bty
BROOKS Sidney	RA	15 AA Bty 8 Coast Regt
BROTHERSTON Andrew	Dockyard Defence Corps	
BROWN David McNeilace	RN	HMS *Tamar*

156

BRYANT Willie	The Middlesex Regt	1st Bn
BRYDIE Cecil C	RN	HMS *Tamar*
BULL Walter	The Middlesex Regt	1st Bn
BURDETT Kenneth	RA	8 Coast Regt
BURGESS Frederick	RA	8 Coast Regt
BURNELL Robert James	HKSRA	1st Bty
BURNETT Alexander Buchan	The Royal Scots	2nd Bn
BURNETT Peter	The Royal Scots	2nd Bn
BURNLEY Fred	RA	965 Defence Bty
BURNS Evan Owen	RA	12th Coast Bty
BURNS Thomas McDermid	The Royal Scots	2nd Bn
BURROWS Edgar George	RN	HMS *Sultan*
BURROWS Frank	RA	12th Coast Bty
BURROWS Vernon Howard	RA	12th Coast Bty
BUTLER Thomas	RA	8 Coast Regt
BUTLER Walter William	RA	8 Coast Regt
CADLE Edward Terence	RA	8 Coast Regt
CALVERT Hans	RN	HMS *Tamar*
CAMPBELL Clifford Herbert Henry	The Middlesex Regt	1st Bn
CAMPBELL James	The Royal Scots	2nd Bn
CAMPBELL William	RN	HMS *Tamar*
CAMPBELL William	RN	HMS *Tamar*
CAMPBELL William	RN	HMS *Tamar*
CARLEY John	RA	965 Defence Bty
CARPENTER Maurice David	RE	40 Fortress Coy
CARRELL George Thomas	The Middlesex Regt	1st Bn
CARRINGTON William	The Royal Scots	2nd Bn
CARTER John Ernest	RE	22 Fortress Coy
CARTER Leslie John	RA	
CARTWRIGHT Leslie George	Royal Signal Corps	HK Signal Coy
CASELEY Frank	RA	8 Coast Regt
CASLAKE Edwin Reginald	The Middlesex Regt	1st Bn
CASSIN Francis	RN	HMS *Thracian*

CHALGRAVE Frank	The Middlesex Regt	1st Bn
CHALMERS Alexander	The Royal Scots	2nd Bn
CHAPMAN Douglas Vernon	The Middlesex Regt	1st Bn
CHARLES Douglas Amos	The Middlesex Regt	1st Bn
CHARLES Sidney	RE	40 Fortress Coy
CHARLTON Rennison	The Royal Scots	2nd Bn
CHEEK George Henry	RN	HMS *Tamar*
CHICK Henry	The Middlesex Regt	1st Bn
CHILCRAFT Robert Albert	RN	
CHILDS Thomas Bernard	RA	
CHOWN George Henry	RA	12th Coast Bty
CHRISTIAN Charles Harold	RA	8 Coast Regt
CHRISTIE George Alexander	The Royal Scots	2nd Bn
CLAPPERTON Robert	The Royal Scots	2nd Bn
CLARK James	The Royal Scots	2nd Bn
CLARK William	The Middlesex Regt	1st Bn
CLARKE Charles Arthur	The Middlesex Regt	1st Bn
CLARKE John Henry	The Middlesex Regt	1st Bn
CLARKE Wilfred Allan	RN	HMS *Tamar*
CLAYTON Samuel	HKSRA	1st Bty
CLEGGETT Albert Ernest	Royal Signal Corps	HK Signal Coy
CLIFFORD George Frederick	The Middlesex Regt	1st Bn
CLOGG George Alfred	RA	12th Coast Bty
COCKBURN Richard	RA	8 Coast Regt
COLE Frederick William	RA	8 Coast Regt
COLEMAN Patrick	The Royal Scots	2nd Bn
COLES Joseph William R	Dockyard Defence Corps	
COLTHORPE Wilfred	RA	8 Coast Regt
COMBE Alexander Hunter	The Royal Scots	2nd Bn
COMMERFORD John	The Middlesex Regt	1st Bn
CONEGHAN James	The Royal Scots	2nd Bn
CONNOLLY John Patrick G	The Middlesex Regt	1st Bn
COOK Henry	The Royal Scots	2nd Bn

COOK James	The Royal Scots	2nd Bn
COOK Peter Harold	Royal Signal Corps	HK Signal Coy
COOKE James Leslie Cyril	RE	40 Fortress Coy
COOKE John Patrick	The Middlesex Regt	1st Bn
COOKE Leonard	RA	965 Defence Bty
COOPER Albert Edward	The Middlesex Regt	1st Bn
COOPER George William	RE	22 Fortress Coy
COPPING Henry George	The Middlesex Regt	1st Bn
CORNWALL Andrew	The Royal Scots	2nd Bn
COUCH Henry	RA	12th Coast Bty
COUSINS George John F	RA	8 Coast Regt
CRABTREE Allan	RN	HMS *Tamar*
CRADDOCK Thomas George	RA	8 Coast Regt
CRANGLE John Raphael	RNVR	HMS *Tamar*
CRAWLEY Frederick William	Royal Signal Corps	Signal Coy
CREED Frederick William	RA	8 Coast Regt
CRICHTON George	The Royal Scots	2nd Bn
CRITTENDEN Albert Stanley	RE	22 Fortress Coy
CROSS William Albert	RA	12th Coast Bty
CROWLEY Patrick Joseph	The Middlesex Regt	1st Bn
CUELL William Tom	RA	8 Coast Regt
CULPECK Francis Henry	The Middlesex Regt	1st Bn
CURTIS Llewellyn	RA	8 Coast Regt
DAINTY George Henry	RA	12th Coast Bty
DAIR Robert Francis	HKSRA	1st Bty
DALY Joseph Hunter	The Royal Scots	2nd Bn
DANNAN Stephen John	Royal Signal Corps	HK Signal Coy
DAVIS Donald Edward	RE	40 Fortress Coy
DAVIS Harold Raymond	RE	22 Fortress Coy
DAVIS John Peter Richard	The Middlesex Regt	1st Bn
DAVIS Joseph William	RA	36 Heavy Bty
DAWES James	The Middlesex Regt	1st Bn
DAWSON George	RE	

DAY Harry	RE	
DELDERFIELD George A	RA	12th Coast Bty
DENYER George	RE	
DICKSON George Jackson	The Royal Scots	2nd Bn
DIXON Norman	RA	8 Coast Regt
DOANE Ernest	RA	8 Coast Regt
DOCHARD John	RA	8 Coast Regt
DODSON Charles Henry	RN	HMS *Tamar*
DONNELLY John	The Royal Scots	2nd Bn
DOOLEY Clifford Vincent	RA	12th Coast Bty
DREW Wilfred	RA	12th Coast Bty
DUCKER Neville James	RN	HMS *Tamar*
DUDDRIDGE Richard Henry	Dockyard Defence Corps	
DUNLOP George	The Royal Scots	2nd Bn
DURIE George Brown	The Royal Scots	2nd Bn
DUROSE Robert James	RA	8 Coast Regt
DUTCH Cecil Henry F	RA	8 Coast Regt
EASTERBROOK William George Ronald	RN	HMS *Tamar*
EATON George	The Middlesex Regt	1st Bn
EDGE Leonard	The Royal Scots	2nd Bn
EDWARDS James Thomas	RA	8 Coast Regt
EDWARDS John E D	RN	HMS *Tamar*
EGAN John	The Royal Scots	2nd Bn
ELLARD Cecil	RA	965 Defence Bty
ELLEY Harold Edward	RA	8 Coast Regt
ELLIOTT Frederick Alexander	The Middlesex Regt	1st Bn
ELLIS Ernest	The Royal Scots	2nd Bn
ELMS David Kenneth	RN	HMS *Tamar*
EMBLETON William	The Royal Scots	2nd Bn
EMBLING James Albert	RE	22 Fortress Coy
EVANS Douglas Charles	RA	8 Coast Regt
EVERETT Leslie Charles	RA	12th Coast Bty
EVES John Charles	RA	8 Coast Regt

FAGE Charles Edward	RN	HMS *Thracian*
FAIRBAIRN Alexander David	The Royal Scots	2nd Bn
FARRIE John Reid	RN	HMS *Tamar*
FERRIE Gordon	Royal Signal Corps	HK Signal Coy
FIDLER Edward Dixon	RA	15 AA Bty 8 Coast Regt
FINCH Harold	RN	HMS *Tamar*
FINCH Richard Howell	RN	HMS *Tamar*
FINDLAY Edward	The Royal Scots	2nd Bn
FISHER Albert Louis	RN	HMS *Tamar*
FISHER Joseph	RA	8 Coast Regt
FISHLOCK Ernest Alfred J	RE	40 Fortress Coy
FLETT Andrew	RNVR	Boom Defence HK
FLINTER Edwin Stuart	RA	35 Bty
FOLEY Andrew	The Middlesex Regt	1st Bn
FORD George	The Royal Scots	2nd Bn
FORD Sidney C	RA	12th Coast Bty
FORSTER Arnold William	RE	40 Fortress Coy
FORSYTH James Leslie Wilson	RN	HMS *Tamar*
FOSS John George	RA	12th Coast Bty
FOSTER Edward Sinclair	RE	22 Fortress Coy
FOX Henry	Royal Signal Corps	HK Signal Coy
FRANCIS Evan Charles	RN	HMS *Tamar*
FRANKLIN John Wilfred	RA	8 Coast Regt
FRENCH Walter Leonard	The Middlesex Regt	1st Bn
FRENCHUM Frank Ernest	The Middlesex Regt	1st Bn
FRY William Francis	RE	40 Fortress Coy
FUDGE John Alfred	RA	12th Coast Bty
FULCHER Cecil Eric	RA	12th Coast Bty
FULLAGAR Albert Oliver	HKSRA	1st Bty
FULLERTON Thomas	The Royal Scots	2nd Bn
FYFFE Neil	The Royal Scots	2nd Bn
GADD George Richard	RA	12th Coast Bty
GAILEY Leonard Henry	RA	8 Coast Regt

GALE Edward George	Royal Signal Corps	HK Signal Coy
GALE John Frederick T	The Middlesex Regt	1st Bn
GALLAGHER Joseph	RA	5 AA Bty
GARDINER George	The Royal Scots	2nd Bn
GARDNER Andrew Pollock	The Royal Scots	2nd Bn
GARRETT Arthur Thomas	RN	HMS *Tamar*
GARTH Patrick	The Royal Scots	2nd Bn
GATES Edwin William	RN	HMS *Tamar*
GENTRY Frederick James	The Middlesex Regt	1st Bn
GEORGE Alfred William	RA	8 Coast Regt
GIBSON Frederick William	The Middlesex Regt	1st Bn
GIBSON Hugh	The Royal Scots	2nd Bn
GIBSON Richard	The Royal Scots	2nd Bn
GILL Norman Henry	RA	8 Coast Regt
GLISTER Montague Henry	RA	8 Coast Regt
GLOVER Herbert Edwin	The Middlesex Regt	1st Bn
GODFREE Ronald Frank	RN	HMS *Tamar*
GODFREY Alfred Trevor	RA	8 Coast Regt
GODSON Austin	The Royal Scots	2nd Bn
GOFF James Henry	RE	22 Fortress Coy
GOLDIE Charles	The Royal Scots	2nd Bn
GOODMAN Albert	The Middlesex Regt	1st Bn
GORDON Ian Francis	The Middlesex Regt	1st Bn
GORMAN James Thomas	Royal Signal Corps	HK Signal Coy
GOUDIE Harold	Royal Signal Corps	HK Signal Coy
GOULD Henry Y J	RA	12th Coast Bty
GOURLAY Ian Douglas	RE	40 Fortress Coy
GRACEY Peter Douglas	Royal Signal Corps	HK Signal Coy
GRAHAM Duncan	RN	HMS *Tamar*
GRAINGER James	The Royal Scots	2nd Bn
GRANT Denis	RE	40 Fortress Coy
GRANT Edward	The Royal Scots	2nd Bn
GRAY Christopher Frederick	RE	22 Fortress Coy

GRAY Frederick Bernard	The Middlesex Regt	1st Bn
GREEN Albert John	RA	8 Coast Regt
GREEN Ernest Edward	Royal Signal Corps	HK Signal Coy
GREEN Frederick	The Middlesex Regt	1st Bn
GREEN Herbert	RN	HMS *Tamar*
GREEN Jack Garfield	RE	22 Fortress Coy
GREEN William Henry	Royal Marines	HMS *Tamar*
GREEN William John	RA	8 Coast Regt
GREENWOOD Norman Thomas John	RN	HMS *Tamar*
GREGORY Thomas Henry	RE	22 Fortress Coy
GREIG William	The Royal Scots	2nd Bn
GREY William Edward	RN	HMS *Tamar*
GRIST Victor Charles	The Middlesex Regt	1st Bn
GUBB Percy William M	The Middlesex Regt	1st Bn
GUILLE John Robert	RA	12th Coast Bty
HAINES Charles Henry	The Middlesex Regt	1st Bn
HALL Douglas James	Royal Signal Corps	HK Signal Coy
HALL Geoffrey Nathaniel	RA	15 AA Bty
HALL Reginald Ernest	The Middlesex Regt	1st Bn
HALL Samuel	The Royal Scots	2nd Bn
HALL Thomas	The Royal Scots	2nd Bn
HALL Walter	RA	965 Defence Bty
HALL Walter John	The Middlesex Regt	1st Bn
HAMILL Thomas	The Royal Scots	2nd Bn
HAMILTON Isaac	The Royal Scots	2nd Bn
HAMMOND Frank	RN	HMS *Tamar*
HANDFORD John Frederick	The Middlesex Regt	1st Bn
HANLEY George	RA	8 Coast Regt
HANNAN Thomas Bernard	RA	12th Coast Bty
HARDINGTON Ronald	RA	12th Coast Bty
HARDY Francis Gordon	RN	
HARE Charles	The Middlesex Regt	1st Bn
HARKINSON William John	Royal Signal Corps	HK Signal Coy

HARPER Henry George	RA	12th Coast Bty
HARPER Ronald George	RN	
HARRIGAN Francis William	RE	22 Fortress Coy
HARRIS Charles Richard	The Middlesex Regt	1st Bn
HARRIS George Arthur	RN	HMS *Tamar*
HARRISON Richard Stuart	RN	RNVR
HART Robert	The Royal Scots	2nd Bn
HARVEY Cyril	The Middlesex Regt	1st Bn
HARVEY James	The Royal Scots	2nd Bn
HATCHETT Percy John	The Middlesex Regt	1st Bn
HATFIELD Charles Henry	The Middlesex Regt	1st Bn
HATTON Thomas	RA	12th Coast Bty
HAVERCROFT Samuel	The Royal Scots	2nd Bn
HAVILAND Charles Stephen	RN	
HAWKINS Joseph Edward	RE	40 Fortress Coy
HAWKINS William Henry	RA	12th Coast Bty
HAWKSWORTH William E J	RN	HMS *Tamar*
HAYNES Harold George	RE	22 Fortress Coy
HAYWARD Walter Alfred	The Middlesex Regt	1st Bn
HEADLEY William Arthur	HKSRA	1st Bty
HEALY Dennis	RN	HMS *Cicala*
HEMMINGFIELD Arthur	RA	15 AA Bty
HENDERSON David	The Royal Scots	2nd Bn
HENDERSON Francis	The Royal Scots	2nd Bn
HENDERSON Lancelot	RA	8 Coast Regt
HENDY Norman	RN	HMS *Tamar*
HESLOP James	RA	12th Coast Bty
HEWER Edward Henry John	Royal Signal Corps	HK Signal Coy
HEWITT Frank	RA	965 Defence Bty
HEWSON Thomas James	RA	965 Defence Bty
HICKMAN Oscar	RA	12th Coast Bty
HILDRED Reginald John	RA	965 Defence Bty
HILL Ernest	RA	8 Coast Regt

HILL George	RN	HMS *Thracian*
HINGE Frank Charles	RN	HMS *Tamar*
HISCOCK Albert Roy	RA	8 Coast Regt
HITCHIN Henry Alfred	RA	8 Coast Regt
HODGE John Henry	Royal Signal Corps	HK Signal Coy
HODGE Walter Resolution	Royal Signal Corps	HK Signal Coy
HODGSON Robert	RN	HMS *Tamar*
HODKINSON Kenneth Townson	The Royal Scots	2nd Bn
HOGAN William	RA	8 Coast Regt
HOLT James Samuel	RN	HMS *Tamar*
HOMBURG John Sydney	RE	40 Fortress Coy
HOOLEY Reginald	RA	8 Coast Regt
HOPE Arthur	The Middlesex Regt	1st Bn
HOPKINS Francis Yonge	RN	HMS *Tamar*
HORNER George Borham	RA	12th Coast Bty
HORSLEY Eric	Royal Marines	HMS *Tamar*
HOSFORD Robert	RN	HMS *Tamar*
HOUGHTON Francis John	The Middlesex Regt	1st Bn
HOWARTH John William	RA	12th Coast Bty
HOWSON Ronald	RN	HMS *Tamar*
HUGHES William	The Royal Scots	2nd Bn
HULL George James Parsons	RN	HMS *Tamar*
HUSBAND Edwin	Royal Signal Corps	HK Signal Coy
HUTCHINSON George William	RN	HMS *Tamar*
HUTCHISON William	The Royal Scots	2nd Bn
HUTTON Edmund Feltham	RN	HMS *Tamar*
ILES Arthur Henry	The Middlesex Regt	1st Bn
IRVING Malcolm	The Royal Scots	2nd Bn
ISAAC Harry	RA	8 Coast Regt
ISZARD George	The Middlesex Regt	1st Bn
JACKSON Albert James	The Middlesex Regt	1st Bn
JACKSON George Allborn Allwood	The Royal Scots	2nd Bn
JALLAND Jack Edward	RN	HMS *Tamar*

JAMES Ivor	The Middlesex Regt	1st Bn
JEFFREY Andrew Buchan	The Royal Scots	2nd Bn
JENKINS Charles	The Royal Scots	2nd Bn
JENKINS, Ernest	The Royal Scots	2nd Bn
JENNING Albert George	The Middlesex Regt	1st Bn
JINKS Henry (Harry)	RA	8 Coast Regt
JOHNS Denzil	HKSRA	1st Bty
JOHNSON Arthur James	RA	12th Coast Bty
JOHNSON Frederick William	RN	HMS *Tamar*
JOHNSON Oliver	RA	15 AA Bty 8 Coast Regt
JOHNSON Wilfred James	RE	40 Fortress Coy
JOHNSTON James	The Royal Scots	2nd Bn
JOHNSTON Robert James	The Royal Scots	2nd Bn
JONES Gonville Royce	RN	HMS *Tamar*
JONES Herbert Cyril	Royal Marines	HMS *Tamar*
JONES James Thomas Alburn	RN	HMS *Tamar*
JONES Thomas David	The Middlesex Regt	1st Bn
JORDAN-BOWDITCH Horace	Royal Signal Corps	HK Signal Coy
JOSLIN Henry John	The Middlesex Regt	1st Bn
KEARNS James Bruce	RN	HMS *Tamar*
KEHOE Edward Michael	RE	40 Fortress Coy
KELLY Maurice	The Royal Scots	2nd Bn
KEMP Stanley	RN	HMS *Tamar*
KENNARD Herbert Walter Godfrey	RN	HMS *Tamar*
KENNEDY Albert	RE	22 Fortress Coy
KENNEDY John Alexander	The Royal Scots	2nd Bn
KENNY Michael	RA	965 Defence Bty
KERRUISH John Alfred	RA	8 Coast Regt
KEW Henry Charles	RN	
KIMBER James	RA	12th Coast Bty
KIMBER Walter William	RN	HMS *Tamar*
KIMPTON William Ernest	RE	22 Fortress Coy
KING Ernest Alfred	RN	HMS *Tamar*

KING John Kenneth	RN	HMS *Tamar*
KINNARD William Henry	RA	8 Coast Regt
KIRBY Alfred	The Royal Scots	2nd Bn
KNOWLES Roland Ernest	RA	12th Coast Bty
KNOX David	RN	RNVR
LAKE Alexander Sidney C McDonald	RE	40 Fortress Coy
LAMB Peter McDonald	The Royal Scots	2nd Bn
LANE Francis Edward	RA	8 Coast Regt
LANE John Hugh	RA	8 Coast Regt
LANGDELL Stanley	The Middlesex Regt	1st Bn
LANGRIDGE Walter Thomas	RA	965 Defence Bty
LAW Reginald	The Middlesex Regt	1st Bn
LAWLOR William John	The Middlesex Regt	1st Bn
LEE Frederick Charles	The Middlesex Regt	1st Bn
LEE Frederick George	RN	HMS *Tamar*
LEES Alexander	RN	HMS *Thracian*
LEIGH Thomas Richard	RA	8 Coast Regt
LEWIS Arthur	Royal Signal Corps	HK Signal Coy
LEWIS Daniel	RN	HMS *Tamar*
LEWIS Ernest	RA	8 Coast Regt
LIFTON Cyril Alfred B	RN	HMS *Tern*
LIMACHER Frank Oliver	RA	8 Coast Regt
LINKLATER Arthur	The Royal Scots	2nd Bn
LINTON James Frederick	RA	8 Coast Regt
LINTOTT George	The Royal Scots	2nd Bn
LITTLE John Thomas	The Middlesex Regt	1st Bn
LITTLEFIELD Frederick	The Middlesex Regt	1st Bn
LIVESEY Albert Charles	RA	7 Bty 5 HAA Regt
LOCHRIE George Sutherland	The Royal Scots	2nd Bn
LOGAN Sydney	The Royal Scots	2nd Bn
LOUGHLIN Peter Harry	HK Police Force	
LOVE Noel John	RA	8 Coast Regt
LUDFORD Arthur Herbert	RN	HMS *Tamar*

LYON George	RA	8 Coast Regt
MACDONALD Thomas	Royal Signal Corps	HK Signal Coy
MACE Frank Edward	RA	965 Defence Bty
MACE Harry Leslie	RA	12th Coast Bty
MACEY Frank Leslie	The Middlesex Regt	1st Bn
MACKAY William	The Royal Scots	2nd Bn
MACKENNY William Henry	RN	HMS *Tamar*
MAIR William	RN	HMS *Robin*
MAKEL George Smith	RA	8 Coast Regt
MANDERS Thomas George	RE	22 Fortress Coy
MANN Charles Henry	RN	HMS *Cicala*
MARRIOTT William Henry	RN	HMS *Tamar*
MARRS William	RN	HMS *Tamar*
MARSH William Thomas	RA	8 Coast Regt
MARSHALL Henry Gibson	The Royal Scots	2nd Bn
MARSHALL Thomas	The Royal Scots	2nd Bn
MARTIN Frank	RN	HMS *Tamar*
MASON William Alfred	RA	12th Coast Bty
MATTHEW Alexander M	The Middlesex Regt	1st Bn
MAY Wilfred	RN	HMS *Tamar*
MAYNARD James Alfred	The Middlesex Regt	1st Bn
MCANDREWS George B	RE	22 Fortress Coy
MCBRIDE Alexander D	RA	12th Coast Bty
MCCALLUM William	The Royal Scots	2nd Bn
MCCORMACK Bernard	RA	8 Coast Regt
MCCULLOCH William	The Royal Scots	2nd Bn
MCDERMOTT Cornelius	The Royal Scots	2nd Bn
MCDERMOTT James	RA	12th Coast Bty
MCDERMOTT Lawrence	RA	8 Coast Regt
MCELROY John	RA	8 Coast Regt
MCENEANEY James	Royal Signal Corps	HK Signal Coy
MCGHEE James Preston	The Royal Scots	2nd Bn
MCGILLIVRAY James	The Royal Scots	2nd Bn

MCGIVNEY John	RA	12th Coast Bty
MCGRATH William Patrick	RN	HMS *Cicala*
MCHUGH Bernard	The Royal Scots	2nd Bn
MCILWRAITH Wilfred Arthur	RE	22 Fortress Coy
MCKINLAY Robert	The Royal Scots	2nd Bn
MCLEAN Andrew Montague	The Royal Scots	2nd Bn
MCLEAN Joseph Henry	RA	12th Coast Bty
MCMEECHAN Hugh McIntosh	The Royal Scots	2nd Bn
MCPHERSON Charles Donald	The Royal Scots	2nd Bn
MCQUEEN George Maclean	RN	HMS *Tamar*
MCSHERRY Peter	The Royal Scots	2nd Bn
MEAD James Charles E	The Royal Scots	2nd Bn
MEDLEY Lloyd Charles	RA	12th Coast Bty
MELBOURNE Frank Edward	The Middlesex Regt	1st Bn
MELLOWS Stephen John	RN	HMS *Tamar*
MELTON John William	RN	HMS *Tamar*
MENDELSON Arthur Leonard	The Middlesex Regt	1st Bn
METCALFE Ernest	Royal Marines	HMS *Tamar*
METCALFE Thomas Arthur	The Middlesex Regt	1st Bn
MILLER Donald	The Royal Scots	2nd Bn
MINCHIN Arthur Felix	RA	8 Coast Regt
MINERS James	RA	965 Defence Bty
MORGAN Trevor Kenneth	Royal Signal Corps	HK Signal Coy
MORRIS Richard	The Royal Scots	2nd Bn
MORRIS William Thomas	The Middlesex Regt	1st Bn
MORRISON Edward	The Middlesex Regt	1st Bn
MORROW William	The Royal Scots	2nd Bn
MORSE Charles John	RN	HMS *Tamar*
MOSE George Alfred	RA	15 AA Bty 8 Coast Regt
MOXHAM Henry Richard	RE	40 Fortress Coy
MURPHY Thomas	The Middlesex Regt	1st Bn
MURRAY John Stuart	The Middlesex Regt	1st Bn
MURRAY William	The Royal Scots	2nd Bn

MURRELL Arthur Robert	The Middlesex Regt	1st Bn
MUSTO Stanley Arthur	HKSRA	1st Bty
NAYLER Herbert Edgar	The Middlesex Regt	1st Bn
NELLIST James	RA	965 Defence Bty
NEWINGTON Richard Thomas John	RE	22 Fortress Coy
NEWMAN Thomas Harry	RE	22 Fortress Coy
NEWNHAM Bertram Charles	Royal Signal Corps	HK Signal Coy
NEWTON Percy Alfred	The Middlesex Regt	1st Bn
NORMAN Alfred William	RA	15 AA Bty 8 Coy
NORTH Albert James	RA	12th Coast Bty
NORTH Frederick Ernest	The Middlesex Regt	1st Bn
O'CONNOR Michael Oliver	The Royal Scots	2nd Bn
O'ROURKE Thomas	The Royal Scots	2nd Bn
O'SULLIVAN Bartholomew	RN	HMS *Thracian*
OAKLEY Thomas Ernest	RA	7 Bty 5 HAA Regt
O'CONNELL Jeremiah	RA	965 Defence Bty
OFFICER John Moore M B	RAMC	27 Coy
OLIVER John Robert	RN	HMS *Tamar*
ORMISTON John Mitchell	The Royal Scots	2nd Bn
ORR Terrance Nolan G	RA	965 Defence Bty
OSMAN Harry James	RN	HMS *Moth*
OSWALD Ronald George	The Middlesex Regt	1st Bn
OUSGOOD Fred	RN	HMS *Tamar*
OWEN George Thomas R	RN	HMS *Tamar*
OWEN Glyn	RA	15 AA Bty 8 Coast Regt
OWEN Gordon John	RA	12th Coast Bty
PACEY Arthur	The Middlesex Regt	1st Bn
PAGE Charles Albert	Royal Signal Corps	HK Signal Coy
PAGE William Cecil	RA	15 AA Bty 8 Coast Regt
PALMER Joseph Benjamin	The Middlesex Regt	1st Bn
PANTING Hugh Eric Randolph	The Middlesex Regt	1st Bn
PAPE George William	The Middlesex Regt	1st Bn
PARKER Raymond John	The Middlesex Regt	1st Bn

PARKINS George Baden	RN	HMS *Tamar*
PARLETTE Reginald George	RN	HMS *Tamar*
PARSONS Arthur John	Royal Signal Corps	HK Signal Coy
PATERSON Henry	The Royal Scots	2nd Bn
PAYNE Arthur	RA	15 AA Bty 8 Coast Regt
PAYNE Terence Robert	The Middlesex Regt	1st Bn
PEARCE Raymond John C	The Middlesex Regt	1st Bn
PEARSON Alfred	The Middlesex Regt	1st Bn
PEARSON Harry	Royal Signal Corps	HK Signal Coy
PEFFERS Adam	The Royal Scots	2nd Bn
PELHAM Harold Alfred G	The Middlesex Regt	1st Bn
PEMBROKE William Henry	RA	8 Coast Regt
PENNICK Reginald Joseph	The Middlesex Regt	1st Bn
PENNY Richard Arthur	The Middlesex Regt	1st Bn
PEPPER Frank Crookes	RE	40 Fortress Coy
PERKINS Leslie George	RN	HMS *Tamar*
PERRY Donald Charles	RE	40 Fortress Coy
PHILIPSON John Beaver	RA	12th Coast Bty
PHILLIPS Reginald Ernest	The Royal Scots	2nd Bn
PHILLIPS Sydney William Ernest	RN	HMS *Tamar*
PHILLIPS, Edward John	The Middlesex Regt	1st Bn
PHIPPS John	Royal Signal Corps	HK Signal Coy
PICKSTON Leslie	Royal Signal Corps	HK Signal Coy
PIKE Horace Henry G	RN	HMS *Cicala*
PLUMMER William Arthur	RA	12th Coast Bty
POLLARD Leonard Hugh	RNVR	HMS *Tamar*
POLLOCK James	The Royal Scots	2nd Bn
POPE Donald Charles	RE	22 Fortress Coy
POTTER Alan Stanley	St John Ambulance	HK Island
POTTER John Henry	Royal Signal Corps	HK Signal Coy
POTTER John Thomas	RA	8 Coast Regt
POTTER Robert	RA	8 Coast Regt
POWELL Albert Victor	RN	HMS *Tamar*

POWELL William John	The Royal Scots	2nd Bn
PRAGNELL Charles	RA	8 Coast Regt
PRESSLEY Harvey	RA	8 Coast Regt
PRIEST Henry Herbert A	RA	12th Coast Bty
PRIEST William James	RNVR	Naval Mine Observation Depot
PRIESTLEY George	RA	12th Coast Bty
PRING Mark Edward	The Middlesex Regt	1st Bn
PRITCHARD James	RA	8 Coast Regt
PROBERT Sidney Charles George	The Middlesex Regt	1st Bn
PRYKE William Arthur J	RN	HMS *Tamar*
PULLAR James	RA	12th Coast Bty
RAINEY Eric	RE	22 Fortress Coy
RAINSFORD Henry Charles	RA	12th Coast Bty
RAMAGE Humphrey George	RE	22 Fortress Coy
RAMSAY John Fitcher	The Royal Scots	2nd Bn
RAMSDEN John Richard	RN	HMS *Tamar*
RAMSEY James Robert	The Middlesex Regt	1st Bn
RANKIN Thomas	RA	12th Coast Bty
RAPER William George	RA	12th Coast Bty
RATCLIFFE Norman Ernest	RE	22 Fortress Coy
RAWLINGS Frank	RA	8 Coast Regt
READ Reginald John	HKRNVR	HMS *Tamar*
REDFERN George Stanley	Royal Signal Corps	HK Signal Coy
REED George William	RA	12th Coast Bty
REES Leonard Frederick	RA	12th Coast Bty
REEVE Sidney Arthur	RE	22 Fortress Coy
REYNOLDS Alfred John	RN	HMS *Tamar*
RICE Thomas	RN	HMS *Tamar*
RICHARDS Frederick W	RAMC	27 Coy
RICHARDS Robert William	The Royal Scots	2nd Bn
RICHARDS Stanley John	RA	8 Coast Regt
RICHARDSON Joseph H	Royal Marines	HMS *Tamar*
RICHES Jack Ernest	The Middlesex Regt	1st Bn

RICHMOND Robert Henry	RE	22 Fortress Coy
RICKETTS George Raymond	RA	8 Coast Regt
RIDDEN Donald	The Middlesex Regt	1st Bn
RITCHIE Robert Hyslop	The Royal Scots	2nd Bn
RITCHINGS Thomas	RA	8 Coast Regt
ROBERTS Alfred Henry	RA	965 Defence Bty
ROBERTS Charles Arthur	RE	40 Fortress Coy
ROBERTS Leonard	The Middlesex Regt	1st Bn
ROBERTSON Albert Thomas	The Middlesex Regt	1st Bn
ROBERTSON Mornington	The Royal Scots	2nd Bn
ROBERTSON Peter Ian N	Royal Signal Corps	HK Signal Coy
ROBINSON Charles	RN	HMS *Tamar*
ROBINSON Henry Charles	RN	HMS *Tamar*
ROBINSON John	RA	8 Coast Regt
ROBINSON Joseph	Royal Signal Corps	HK Signal Coy
ROBINSON Percy Albert George	RE	40 Fortress Coy
RODGERS Stephen Patrick	RN	HMS *Tamar*
ROGERS Ernest James W	RA	8 Coast Regt
ROGERS John Francis	Royal Signal Corps	HK Signal Coy
ROMPEN George	The Royal Scots	2nd Bn
ROOKER Roy Leslie Harold	The Middlesex Regt	1st Bn
ROOS Victor Edward	RN	HMS *Tamar*
ROSS John Connacher	The Royal Scots	2nd Bn
ROUND Walter Thomas	RA	8 Coast Regt
RULE Albert	The Middlesex Regt	1st Bn
RULE Charles Frederick	The Middlesex Regt	1st Bn
RUSHMAN Mervyn Francis	Royal Marines	HMS *Tamar*
RUSSELL Alexander	The Royal Scots	2nd Bn
RUSSELL Reginald Edward	The Middlesex Regt	1st Bn
RUSSELL Robert	The Middlesex Regt	1st Bn
RUSSELL Thomas	RA	965 Defence Bty
SAMUELS Christopher	The Middlesex Regt	1st Bn
SANSUM Harry	The Middlesex Regt	1st Bn

SAWYER William Arthur	RN	HMS *Tamar*
SAYCE Thomas	RA	12th Coast Bty
SCHORSCH Robert	The Middlesex Regt	1st Bn
SCOTT Alexander C	The Royal Scots	2nd Bn
SCOTT Arthur Reginald G	RE	22 Fortress Coy
SCOTT Donald	The Royal Scots	2nd Bn
SCOTT Frank Douglas	RA	12th Coast Bty
SCOTT Robert Ferrie	The Royal Scots	2nd Bn
SCULLY John Patrick	Royal Signal Corps	HK Signal Coy
SEAGER Albert Ernest	RA	8 Coast Regt
SEARLE Henry George A	HKSRA	1st Bty
SELWOOD George William	RA	8 Coast Regt
SERCOMBE William Morley	RN	HMS *Tamar*
SHARP Duncan	RA	12th Coast Bty
SHARP Henry Thomas	RN	HMS *Tamar*
SHARROCK Harold Maynard	The Royal Scots	2nd Bn
SHEPHERD George	RA	8 Coast Regt
SHEPHERD Thomas William	Royal Signal Corps	HK Signal Coy
SHERMAN Soloman	RN	HMS *Tern*
SHIELDS Thomas Perkins	RN	HMS *Tamar*
SHIPP Cecil Edward	RE	40 Fortress Coy
SHIRKEY John Dollar	RN	HMS *Tern*
SHIRLAW George Fitness	RA	8 Coast Regt
SHIRLEY Ernest Francis	RA	965 Defence Bty
SHORT Leslie Charles	The Middlesex Regt	1st Bn
SIMMONDS Harold Augustine Pearce	RN	HMS *Tamar*
SIMMONS Edward Walter	RE	22 Fortress Coy
SIMPSON Thomas	The Middlesex Regt	1st Bn
SIMPSON Matthew Allen	RA	7 Bty 5 HAA
SINCLAIR Frederick Leonard	The Middlesex Regt	1st Bn
SINGLETON Thomas	RE	40 Fortress Coy
SKINNER John	The Royal Scots	2nd Bn
SMALE Albert Edward	RN	HMS *Tamar*

SMALLEY Frank	The Middlesex Regt	1st Bn
SMITH Albert Edward	RA	12th Coast Bty
SMITH Ernest Alexander	The Middlesex Regt	1st Bn
SMITH Frederick William	RA	12th Coast Bty
SMITH John Brazier	HKSRA	1st Bty
SMITH John Peter	RA	7 Bty 5 HAA
SMITH Leslie Frank	RE	40 Fortress Coy
SMITH Leslie Ivor	RA	8 Coast Regt
SMITH Matthew	The Royal Scots	2nd Bn
SMITH Patrick	The Royal Scots	2nd Bn
SPALL Arthur Ernest	The Middlesex Regt	1st Bn
SPARE Dermot	Royal Signal Corps	HK Signal Coy
SPARKES John Charles	RA	8 Coast Regt
SPENCE John Frederick	RE	40 Fortress Coy
SPENCER Geoffrey William	RE	40 Fortress Coy
SPENCER Reginald Charles	RE	22 Fortress Coy
SPIERS George Edward	The Middlesex Regt	1st Bn
STANCER Frank Lewis	The Royal Scots	2nd Bn
STANFORD Frederick (Sammy)	The Royal Scots	2nd Bn
STANNERS Adam Ramsey	The Royal Scots	2nd Bn
STEED Thomas	Royal Naval Auxiliary Sick Berth Reserve	HMS *Tamar*
STEELE William Ernest	The Middlesex Regt	1st Bn
STEMP Reginald Stanley	RA	8 Coast Regt
STEWART Forbes	The Royal Scots	2nd Bn
STEWART William	The Middlesex Regt	1st Bn
STEWART William Gallagher	The Royal Scots	2nd Bn
STICKLEY Thomas	The Middlesex Regt	1st Bn
STOBBART John Douglas	RA	12th Coast Bty
STOCKER James Lawrence	RA	8 Coast Regt
STOKER Ralph William	RNVR	HMS *Tamar*
STONE George Frederick	RA	8 Coast Regt
STONE Thomas John	RN	HMS *Tamar*
STOTT James Black	Royal Signal Corps	HK Signal Coy

STURDY Patrick Joseph	The Middlesex Regt	1st Bn
SUGGITT Robert	Royal Signal Corps	HK Signal Coy
SUMNER William	RA	965 Defence Bty
SWEENEY Daniel Christopher	RN	HMS *Tamar*
TAIT Alexander	The Middlesex Regt	1st Bn
TAIT Robert	The Royal Scots	2nd Bn
TALKS Vernon	Royal Signal Corps	HK Signal Coy
TARNER John Norman	The Middlesex Regt	1st Bn
TAYLOR Alec	The Middlesex Regt	1st Bn
TAYLOR Gerald Francis	RAMC	Attached support unit
TAYLOR Norman	RA	12th Coast Bty
TAYLOR Sydney George	Merchant Navy	Former RNVR
TAYLOR Sydney John	RN	HMS *Tamar*
THACKERAY Samuel Robert	RA	8 Coast Regt
THOMAS Alfred Llewellyn	RE	22 Fortress Coy
THOMAS Cyril	The Middlesex Regt	1st Bn
THOMAS Edwin	RA	8 Coast Regt
THOMAS Jack	The Middlesex Regt	1st Bn
THOMAS Jack Henry	The Middlesex Regt	1st Bn
THOMPSON Andrew	The Royal Scots	2nd Bn
THOMPSON Frederick John	RA	12th Coast Bty
THOMPSON William	RE	40 Fortress Coy
THOMSON Alexander	The Royal Scots	2nd Bn
THOMSON David Haston	The Royal Scots	2nd Bn
THORN Ronald Alfred	RE	22 Fortress Coy
THRUSH James Waters	RA	8 Coast Regt
TIVEY Richard John	The Middlesex Regt	1st Bn
TOMLINSON John Bramley	Royal Signal Corps	HK Signal Coy
TOOLEY Michael	RA	30 Bty
TOWNSEND George	RA	965 Defence Bty
TOZER Stanley Herbert	RN	HMS *Tamar*
TRINDER George	The Royal Scots	2nd Bn
TUCKER Joseph Henry	The Middlesex Regt	1st Bn

TUNMER William Arthur	The Middlesex Regt	1st Bn
TURNBULL James	RE	22 Fortress Coy
TURNER Frank	RE	22 Fortress Coy
TURNER William Arthur	RN	HMS *Tamar*
TWOMEY Wilfred Roy	RE	40 Fortress Coy
UPTON Edward George Henry	RE	40 Fortress Coy
VALENTINE George F W	RN	HMS *Tamar*
VALENTINE Roland Edward	The Middlesex Regt	1st Bn
VALLANCE George William Bernard	The Middlesex Regt	1st Bn
VIOTTO Joseph	RA	965 Defence Bty
WADDINGTON Wilfred Gibson	RA	8 Coast Regt
WAKEFIELD Joseph William	The Royal Scots	2nd Bn
WALKER Frederick Charles	The Middlesex Regt	1st Bn
WALKER Leighton William David	The Royal Scots	2nd Bn
WALKER William	The Royal Scots	2nd Bn
WALLACE Warner	RA	8 Coast Regt
WALTERS John	The Royal Scots	2nd Bn
WARBURTON John	RA	12th Coast Bty
WARD Bernard M J	RA	8 Coast Regt
WARDER Alexander Charles	RA	12th Coast Bty
WARREN Christopher	Royal Signal Corps	HK Signal Coy
WATERS Robert Edward	The Middlesex Regt	1st Bn
WATHEN Walter Norman	Royal Signal Corps	HK Signal Coy
WATKINS John Patrick	The Middlesex Regt	1st Bn
WATSON Arthur	RN	RNVR
WATSON Thomas	RA	8 Coast Regt
WEAVER John Douglas Haig	The Middlesex Regt	1st Bn
WEBB Donald	RN	HMS *Tamar*
WEBB Sidney	RN	HMS *Tamar*
WEBSTER Allan	The Middlesex Regt	1st Bn
WEBSTER George	RA	8 Coast Regt
WEEKS Douglas Reginald	Royal Signal Corps	HK Signal Coy
WELLINGTON Richard Henry	RA	7 Bty 5 HAA

WELLS William George	RA	8 Coast Regt
WELSH James Blaney	The Royal Scots	2nd Bn
WESTON John William	RE	40 Fortress Coy
WEXHAM Robert Martin	RN	HMS *Tamar*
WHELAN William	RE	22 Fortress Coy
WHITE Ralph James	RN	HMS *Tamar*
WHITE Robert	The Royal Scots	2nd Bn
WHITEFIELD Charles Arthur	Royal Signal Corps	HK Signal Coy
WHITEHEAD Arthur F	RA	8 Coast Regt
WHITEHOUSE Herbert	The Middlesex Regt	1st Bn
WHITHAM James Percival	The Middlesex Regt	1st Bn
WIGZELL Wallace Frank	Royal Signal Corps	HK Signal Coy
WILLIAMS Frederick Ivor	RA	8 Coast Regt
WILLIAMS Harry Edward Iles	RN	HMS *Tamar*
WILLIAMS Ronald Frederick	RA	8 Coast Regt
WILLIAMS Thomas Alun	RE	22 Fortress Coy
WILLIAMSON James	The Royal Scots	2nd Bn
WILLIS Francis	Royal Signal Corps	HK Signal Coy
WILSON Arthur Stanley	RA	8 Coast Regt
WILSON Charles Edward	The Royal Scots	2nd Bn
WILSON John Campbell	RN	HMS *Thracian*
WILSON William Eric	RA	8 Coast Regt
WITHINGTON Henry	RA	12th Coast Bty
WITTY Herbert Charles	The Middlesex Regt	1st Bn
WOOD Lawrence Arthur	The Middlesex Regt	1st Bn
WOOLDRIDGE Edward	RA	8 Coast Regt
WOOLLCOTT Edgar Joseph	RE	40 Fortress Coy
WOOLLEY Bertram	The Middlesex Regt	1st Bn
WOOLWRIGHT Alfred	The Royal Scots	2nd Bn
WORDLEY Ernest George	RAMC	27 Coy
WYLIE William	The Royal Scots	2nd Bn
YEOMAN Herbert George	RA	965 Defence Bty

Bibliography[135]

Hong Kong Changsha Combat War History Collection 47. Japan: Japanese Ministry of Defence Asagumo News, 1971

Shōwa History. Japan: Mainichi Shinbun, 1971.

The Sea Bears Witness. China: Zhoushan City Chinese Communist Party Committee Propaganda Department, 2006.

Tony Banham. *The Sinking of the "Lisbon Maru": Britain's Forgotten Wartime Tragedy*. Hong Kong: Hong Kong University Press, 2006.

Tony Banham. *Not the Slightest Chance: The Defence of Hong Kong 1941*. Hong Kong: Hong Kong University Press, 2003.

Alan Birch and Martin Cole. *Captive Christmas: The Battle of Hong Kong, December 1941*. UK: Heinemann, 1984.

G B Endacott and A Birch. *Hong Kong Eclipse*. UK: Oxford University Press (China) Ltd, 1978.

Ted Ferguson. *Desperate Siege: the Battle of Hong Kong*. Canada: Doubleday and Co, 1980.

Ogura Guangsheng. *Hong Kong*. Japan: Iwanami Shoten, 1942.

Masanuri Ito. *Assumed Enemy*. Japan: Sasaki Publishing Department, 1926.

Ko Tim-keung and Tong Cheuk-man. *Japanese Occupation of Hong Kong*. Hong Kong: Joint Publishing Company, 1995.

Kwan Lai Hung. *Hong Kong in the Period of Japanese Occupation*. Hong Kong: Joint Publishing Company, 1993.

Li Shu Fan. *Hong Kong Surgeon*. Hong Kong: Li Shu Fan Medical Fund, 1965.

Oliver Lindsay. *At the Going Down of the Sun – Hong Kong and South East Asia 1941-45*. UK: Hamish Hamilton, 1981.

Oliver Lindsay. *The Lasting Honour: the Fall of Hong Kong 1941*. UK: Hamish Hamilton,1978.

Maj Gen CM Maltby. *Despatch on Operations in Hong Kong from 8th to 25th Dec 1941*. UK: Supplement to the *London Gazette*, 27 January 1948.

Gregory F Michno. *Death on the Hellships: Prisoners at Sea in the Pacific War*. USA: US Naval Institute Press; 1st ed. (US) edition June 2001.

Edwin Ride. *BAAG: Hong Kong Resistance 1942-1945*. UK: Oxford University Press, 1981.

D Rollo. *The Guns and Gunners of Hong Kong.* UK: Gunners' Roll of Hong Kong, 1992.

Sa Kongliao. *Record of Hong Kong under Japanese Occupation.* Hong Kong: Joint Publishing Company, 1946.

Tong Hoi. *Record of Hong Kong's Enemy Occupation.* China: Sunsun Publishing Company Shanghai 1946.

Internet References

Canada at War.
wwii.ca/index.php?page=Page&action=showpage&id=32[136]
Dongji 1942 – History has not sunk.
zjnews.zjol.com.cn/05zjnews/system/2005/08/10/006265410.shtml^
Dongji Rescue. http://www.dongjidao.com/lisbonmaru/^
Hong Kong War Diary. www.hongkongwardiary.com/
Japanese Navy at Guadalcanal 1942.
www.magweb.com/sample/ww2/co01guao.htm* *Lt Geoffrey C Hamilton.*
scotsatwar.co.uk/veteransreminiscences/gchamilton.htm*
Lisbon Maru. en.wikipedia.org/wiki/Lisbon_Maru
Lisbon Maru Association. www.lisbonmarufoundation.org/*
"Lisbon Maru" Remaining Doubts. Xinhua Net.
www.zj.xinhuanet.com/magazine/2006-07/18/content_7548196.htm^*
"Lisbon Maru" Sinking. BBC Hong Kong:
www.bbc.co.uk/ww2peopleswar/categories/c55325/*
Phoenix Explores the Mysteries – Japanese shipwreck.
www.phoenixtv.com/phoenixtv/74323730452447232/index.shtml^
Roll of Honour: Britain at War. www.roll-of-honour.org.uk/Hell_Ships/Lisbon_Maru/
Sinking of the "Lisbon Maru" Historical Research
www.lisbonmaru.org/[137]
The "Lisbon Maru" - Britain's Forgotten Wartime Tragedy.
www.lisbonmaru.com/

The Sinking of the "Lisbon Maru". www.fepow-community.org.uk/arthur_lane/html/sinking_of_the_lisbo n_maru.htm*

Zhejiang Online News Website. www.zjol.com.cn^#

Key to Symbols
(added by the Translator and used in the list of Internet References above)

^ Chinese language websites
* websites no longer valid
# links leading to the home page of Chinese websites, not to any specific article

Additional Material

Route of escape taken by AJW Evans
after the torpedoing of the *Lisbon Maru*[138]

The following account, which is not part of the original Chinese book translated here, was brought to the attention of the translator by Elizabeth Ride, daughter of the late Sir Lindsay Ride CBE, from the collection of his papers, and is transcribed with the kind permission of the National Archives, Kew. It provides contemporaneous material about the personal experiences of the three prisoners Evans, Fallace and Johnstone during their escape and travels across China, and complements the account provided in this translation by Miao Kaiyun's daughter, Miao Zhifen, in the chapter 'Oral account of history: "Father did what Chinese people should do"'.

***

The *Lisbon Maru* was torpedoed at 7.00am on the morning of 2 October. Whether we were towed after the torpedoing is not known – efforts were made to tow us as we heard tow ropes snap, but how much towing was effected is unknown while how much we drifted after the torpedoing is also unknown. Land was visible in the distance on the port side of the ship which was going north, and after the ship sank, I was in the water for between three and four hours, swimming steadily towards land being helped considerably by a very strong tide sweeping towards land. According to the Chinese who rescued me, the *Lisbon Maru* sank about twenty Li from the island – between six and seven miles. I was picked out of the sea after I had swum between two islands, looking for a place to land, by Chinese fishermen, who took me to their home on the largest island, and it was on this island that I was hidden – together with Johnstone and Fallace – and from which we were finally rescued by guerrillas.

The name of this island is Tsing-Pan and is one of the fifty-three islands that make up the Chusan Archipelago. We remained hidden on Tsing-Pan for six days i.e. from 2 to 6 October. On 8 October we were informed that we were to leave as guerrillas had come to help us. We left about 1pm on 8 October by small junk and arrived mid-night at another island, had a hurried meal and then left the island by another beach in a large junk and sailed for some hours, arriving early in the morning on the island of

Wooloo. After another hurried meal we walked overland some six or seven miles, were met at a small village by a band of guerrillas. We were then put in chairs and carried another six or seven miles, where we met more guerrillas and boarded a very large sea going junk, leaving the island of Wooloo. After a junk journey of some four or five hours, we reached what I believe was the mainland, and en route had a very narrow escape from a Japanese destroyer. However, on reaching the mainland we had a journey across country of some ten miles, arriving at the guerrilla headquarters at a place called Kuochu about 6pm on 9 October. Here we met the local guerrilla leader Wong Kyi Nun and stayed with him for three days, being very warmly welcomed, and getting our first hot bath for ten months, clean clothes and marvellous food. Our clothes were Chinese and made hurriedly by a Chinese tailor whom Wong Kyi Nun called in for us.

We left Wong on 13th and guarded always by a band of guerrillas were carried by chair over mountainous country by day and night, visiting en route another guerrilla leader Chu Tieh Chun whose headquarters were in a large temple in the densely woody mountains. Then we were taken to the sea again, and had our last junk journey up a large estuary, which is clearly marked on all maps, finally arriving at Changtse. This is a very small town and is difficult to find on maps, but after spending a day here with General Su Bun Sun – the officer in command of Chinese National Army troops in this area – we went on by chair to Lian Wang (also called Ninghai) and were received and looked after by Commissioner Hsu Tsun arriving here on 16 October.

From here we cabled the British Embassy in Chungking, informing them of our escape and asking them for route instructions and funds for our trip to Chungking. Instead of waiting here for Chungking's reply, we were sent on to Linhai (old name Taichowfu), leaving Lian Wang on 19 October, staying the night at Barzien en route, arriving at Linhai (Taichowfu) about noon on 21 October. Here we stayed at the home Mr and Mrs Frank Englund, of the China Inland Mission, for two weeks, receiving marvellous hospitality and unforgettable kindness, while we also received much needed medical attention. (Incidentally, Mr and Mrs Englund looked after five badly wounded American airmen who had bombed Tokyo, as these men were taken to Linhai by the Chinese who found their wrecked plane – one of the men was Capt Lawson, author of *30 Seconds Over Tokyo*. At Linhai we received very courteous treatment from the Magistrate Mr Chuang Ching Hua.

We moved on from Linhai on 7 November, acting on instructions received from the British Embassy Chunking, and the first big city we reached was Wenchow, passing en route Haimen, Hwan Yeng which we reached by steam launch. Then by canal boat we passed through Liuchiao and Hwan Ling. From Hwan Ling to Hwan Ling Gar, Dar, Tsing, Hwang Chiao and Ngok Ching by chair, and then from Ngok Ching, first by canal boat until the river was reached, then we changed into a junk arriving at Wenchow at about 10pm on 11 November. Here we stayed until the morning of 13 November, meeting amongst other officials Mr Chang Pang Sun – a very senior and well known official of the Chekiang Province. We left Wenchow on 13 November by river boat, being towed in a "boat train" by steam launch. Arrived at Ching Tian that evening, leaving early next morning by river boat, making slow progress owing to the shallow water, the boat being poled and also pulled by rope. We passed through Jaio Foo, arriving at Lishui on the evening of 15 November.

We left Lishui on the morning of 17 November by river boat, passing lovely scenery as we had since leaving Wenchow, and arrived at Pi Yu, here meeting a Maj Lankester of the British Military Mission. We left the next day 18th at noon, in river boat spending one night on the boat, and arrived at a small village where a small bus was sent for us, and we arrived at Yung Ho at 6pm on 19 November. We stayed at Yung Ho until 1 pm on 21 November, leaving by motor car and here we said au revoir to Mr Liu Ting Pao who had been our guide and friend right from Linhai, to which place he now returned. After driving over mountainous roads, amongst magnificent scenery, we arrived at Leung Chwang at 4pm on 21 November. We had now hit the bus route and left Leung Chwang by motorbus, arriving at Pu Chen in Fukien Province at 11am on 22 November. Left here next morning by bus arriving at Chen Yang at 1pm on 23 November after scare from Jap planes en route and were met here by Capt Hardy of the British Military Mission at Chungking. We stayed at

Cheng Yang until the morning of 27 November, where we were accommodated for two nights by Mr and Mrs Bankhardt – American missionaries. (I believe this place is also referred to as Pen Ping). Left Nan Ping by bus 6am on 29 November arriving at Yungan, and Bangkan (small village) and finally reaching Chang Ting, on 1 December, leaving here by postal motor bus at 6am on 3 December and arriving Kan Hsien 8pm on 3 December. Stayed here till 6am on 5 December. (Kukong or Jukong is, I believe, now called Suichow and is the wartime capital of Kwangtung as Canton is in Jap hands).

From Kukong leaving there 10 December, we went by train to Kweilin arriving there on 11 December and from here we were flown in an American transport plane to Kunming. We stayed at the Headquarters of the British Military Mission (OC Col Ride) in Kweilin until 16 December, when we flew to Kunming. At Kunming we separated, the other two going to India, while I was instructed to fly to Chungking, where I arrived on 22 December, again being flown by the American Air Force from Kunming to Chungking on 22 December. This time I had the honour of flying with General Chenault. I should mention that at Kunming we were interrogated by the American Bomber Command Officers, and other intelligence officers, about our trip, while we were able to give some useful information on the movement of ships and use of harbour etc by the Japs in Hongkong. From Chungking, which I left on 26 December, I flew to Calcutta, and all the way to Baltimore by air.

Abbreviations
used by the translator in the translation of the Chinese-language book,
A Faithful Record of the "Lisbon Maru" Incident

2Lt	2nd Lieutenant (or Second Lieutenant)
AA	Anti-Aircraft
BEM	British Empire Medal
Bn	Battalion
Brig	Brigadier
Bty	Battery
Capt	Captain
Col	Colonel
Coy	Company (military term)
Gen	General
HAA	Heavy Anti-aircraft
HK	Hong Kong
HKSRA	Hong Kong Singapore Royal Artillery
HMS	His Majesty's Ship
HQ	Headquarters
LCDR	Lieutenant Commander (US Navy)
L Cdr	Lieutenant Commander (Royal Navy)
Lcol	Lieutenant Colonel (Canadian Army)
Lieut	Lieutenant (US Forces)
Lt	Lieutenant (British Forces)
Lt Col	Lieutenant (British Army)
Lt Gen	Lieutenant General
Maj	Major
Maj Gen	Major General
MBE	Member of the Most Excellent Order of the British Empire
MC	Military Cross
MSc	Master of Science
No.	Number
NYK	Nippon Yusen Kabushiki-Kaisha
OSK	Osaka Shosen Kaisha
PID	Political Intelligence Department
POW	Prisoner of War
RA	Royal Artillery

RAMC	Royal Army Medical Corps
RE	Royal Engineers
Regt	Regiment
Ret'd	Retired
RIASC	Royal Indian Army Service Corps
RN	Royal Navy
RNVR	Royal Naval Volunteer Reserve
SAR	Special Administrative Region
UK	United Kingdom
US	United States
USN	United States Navy
USS	United States Ship
WO	Warrant Officer

Additional Abbreviations
used in the "Additional Material"

Jap	Japanese
OC	Officer Commanding

Statistics

The statistics used in the original Chinese book about the prisoners of war on the ship and what happened to them are not reliable. Tony Banham, author of, *The Sinking of the "Lisbon Maru": Britain's Forgotten Wartime Tragedy*, has said he believes they were drawn from the Japanese wartime propaganda newspaper, the English language *Hong Kong News*. The figures given in Appendix 3 to Tony Banham's book have been carefully researched and should be given credibility. His figures are given in the notes at the end of this volume. In summary, Banham states that 1,834 prisoners of war were put onto the *Lisbon Maru* in Hong Kong; 1,006 survived the incident, including those rescued by the Chinese; and 828 perished.

The Chinese seem to have kept accurate records for those they rescued, which totalled 384.

Chinese names

Chinese names are of course written in Chinese characters, not Roman letters. There are various systems of Romanisation to try to represent how these characters are pronounced. Although all Chinese use the same characters (but see separate section below on Translating from Chinese for further details), they are pronounced quite differently in different dialects (which are virtually different languages). In this book, most names are rendered in the *pinyin* system used in mainland China, which gives some idea of how the characters are pronounced in Mandarin, the official Chinese language. Names of those from Hong Kong are given in the Sidney Lau system of Romanisation, which attempts to represent the pronunciation in Cantonese, the *lingua franca* of Hong Kong.

A Chinese name usually consists of three characters, although it can be two or four in some cases. The surname is always the first character. A married woman often puts her husband's surname first, followed by her maiden surname.

Many of the Hong Kong names in this book are given in the version by which they are commonly known in English, such as Nelson Mar.

Place names

The place names in this book are confusing and need a little explanation.

Zhoushan is an archipelago with many islands. It is also a city as an administrative structure, with the other towns and islands under its jurisdiction.

Dongji is the name of a township within Zhoushan. Under the jurisdiction of Dongji Township are the three islands, Miaozihu, Qingbang and Xifushan. It is to these three islands that the prisoners of war were taken when they were rescued. The name, "Dongji" means "extreme east", because the group of islands is indeed the most easterly part of China; although curiously the island on which Dongji Town sits (Miaozihu), is not actually the most eastern.

The name Dongji is also often used to refer to Miaozihu Island, and because of the special meaning of its name, it is also sometimes used to refer to the group of islands more generally.

The book includes an aerial photograph showing these islands.

Recent events

Since the Chinese book, *A Faithful Record of the "Lisbon Maru" Incident* was published in 2007, the *Lisbon Maru* Association of Hong Kong has maintained and developed strong relations with Zhoushan. Their contacts include members of the local government, the *Lisbon Maru* Research Society in Zhoushan and the Zhejiang Ocean University. They work together to help keep alive the memory of this Incident.

The Dongji Museum of History and Culture opened in 2010 and is largely dedicated to exhibits connected with the events of October 1942.

Commemorative events have been held annually in Zhoushan in October, to pay tribute to the courage of the fishermen who carried out the rescue in 1942, and to remember the souls of the 828 who still lie at the bottom of the ocean off Dongji Island.

The *Lisbon Maru* Association of Hong Kong has played a significant role in organising these events. A major commemoration was held in 2012, the 70th Anniversary of the sinking.

In remembering the souls of the dead, the people of Zhoushan now wear poppies. This is due directly to the influence of Kent Shum of the *Lisbon Maru* Association of Hong Kong. Many Chinese people are puzzled by the British habit of wearing poppies for Remembrance Day and believe that this somehow has links to the Opium Wars and is therefore an anti-Chinese gesture. It is gratifying that Kent Shum has started to correct this wholly false impression, at least in one corner of China.

The year 2015 saw a number of events to mark the Anniversary of the sinking.

In September, the London Chinese Philharmonic Choir held a concert in Cadogan Hall in London to commemorate the 70th Anniversary of the Victory of the Second World War and the War of Resistance Against Japan. The programme mainly consisted of wartime songs from both the Pacific and European theatres of war, and featured the first performance in the UK of the Yellow River Cantata. I was honoured to be asked to give a talk describing the *Lisbon Maru* Incident, the courage of the fishermen and the sad fate of those who perished. This was followed by a piano performance of Ian Parkinson's, the 'Hymn of the *Lisbon Maru*', played by Emas Au (欧惠雯). The story and the haunting music moved the audience to tears. Many commented later that they found this a very moving and tragic story.

In October the usual commemorative events were held in Zhoushan, this time at the Zhejiang Ocean University. Poppy wreaths provided by the Royal British Legion (Hong Kong and China Branch) were presented on behalf of the Royal British Legion (Hong Kong and China Branch), the Hong Kong Prisoners of War Association, the British Consulate General in Hong Kong, and others.

Also in 2015, on 20 October, during his State Visit to the United Kingdom, President Xi Jinping made reference to the *Lisbon Maru* Incident in the speech that he gave at the State Banquet held in his honour in Buckingham Palace, when he said, "During the Second World War, fishermen from Zhoushan in China's Zhejiang Province risked their lives to rescue hundreds of British prisoners of war from the Japanese ship *Lisbon Maru*." and he went on to stress that the sharing of friendship in the flames of war became, "a treasure in bilateral relations".

Although Charles Jordan has now passed away, the people of Zhoushan still remember his visit in 2005, and were keen to keep in touch with his widow, the ninety-five-year-old Mrs Doreen Jordan. In November, Mr Hu Mu, captain of the *Green Eyebrows* sailing-boat, presented to Kent Shum a stone from Dongji, asking him to send it to Mrs Jordan as a memento. Kent got his son, Cardiff, to paint the stone with the Chinese characters for "Dongji Island" (東極島) and prepared a Perspex presentation box with an inscription in both Chinese and English. I was visiting Hong Kong at the time and he asked me to deliver it to Mrs Jordan. I arrived back in the UK on the morning of 11 November, Armistice Day, and went to see her. Mrs Jordan, her two sons and a daughter were all at her house, as were representatives of *Panda Online* TV and Vivian Ni, a reporter from the *Zhoushan News* Media Group. We gathered for the customary two minutes silence and I then presented Mrs Jordan with the stone. She and her family were very moved by the gesture of the gift from Zhoushan.

Mrs Jordan wrote a letter to President Xi to thank him for referring to the *Lisbon Maru* Incident during his speech, and for having authorised the 2005 visit by her late husband and the family, which he had done when he was Party Secretary of Zhejiang Province. (Sadly, Mrs Jordan has since passed away.)

The second of October 2017 marked the 75th Anniversary of the sinking of the *Lisbon Maru*. Commemorative events were held on this day both in Zhoushan and in London. The event in China was organised by the East China Sea Development Institute of the Zhejiang Ocean University in Zhoushan. The Institute held a seminar in the evening in Zhoushan to coincide with the memorial ceremony taking place in London. Both events were filmed by Chinese television companies and a live link made it possible for participants to talk to each other across the world, [139] including a conversation with one of the elderly fishermen who took part in the rescue in 1942, Mr Lin Agen. As well as local tributes, wreaths were laid by the *Lisbon Maru* Association of Hong Kong on behalf of the British Consulate General in Hong Kong, the Royal British Legion (Hong Kong and China Branch), the Hong Kong Prisoners of War Association and the Princess of Wales's Royal Regiment. The organiser of this event, Mr Hu Mu, delivered an Oration in Chinese, and I read out an English translation at the event in London. Hu said:

"Today, we here solemnly grieve for the 800 allied comrades-in-arms who fought shoulder-to-shoulder with us in the Asia Pacific Campaign.

"Seventy-five years ago, on 2 October 1942, the massacre of the sinking of the *Lisbon Maru* took place in the seas of the Zhoushan archipelago. At that time, the *Lisbon Maru*, which had been refitted as a transport ship, was sailing from Hong Kong towards Japan, fully loaded with 1,816 British prisoners of war as well as goods and materials. En route, as it was passing Dongji in Zhoushan waters, it was sunk by an American submarine. During the time when the *Lisbon Maru* was sinking, not only did the Japanese soldiers fail to carry out a rescue, they also cruelly confined the prisoners of war in the ship's holds, in an effort to create the false impression that the American forces had slaughtered the prisoners of war. Then they used machine-guns and rifles to kill the prisoners of war who had made a break-out, with the result that more than eight hundred British officers and men died, from being shot by Japanese soldiers or swallowed up by the sea.

"Soldiers of all nations who rushed to the front in the War of Resistance against Japan were above national and party struggles and put aside religious differences to resist external aggression. The flower of youth fought in the flames of war with a strong esprit de corps; these were real soldiers! Some were buried where they lay; others came back in coffins. As for the survivors, some returned home with honour, some became destitute and homeless, some are old and frail. And here, the eight hundred British servicemen who have long been sleeping on the seabed struggled to the death against the Japanese army to defend their national dignity. Although they fell, they did not yield: they built a monument with their flesh and blood, in the foreign land of the Zhoushan archipelago, forgotten by their country with the passage of history.

"During the Second World War, Japanese militarism carried out unforgivable war crimes against their prisoners of war and civilians. Although Japanese militarism ended in defeat in the Second World War, the governments and peoples of all Asian countries still need to retain a clear-headed understanding of it. Therefore, we here today hold a memorial ceremony to honour these foreign servicemen with sincere hearts and the strength of people-to-people feeling. We shall mark this hidden piece of history to bring solace to the spirits of the forgotten battlefield heroes and shine a light on their glory and dignity. Lest we forget, always cherish the memory.

"Even now, at this memorial ceremony for the 75th Anniversary of the sinking of the *Lisbon Maru*, always remember the true facts of history, carry forward the spirit of the War of Resistance and send forth the sounds of peace.

"Let us work together for tolerance, human kindness amongst people, and Heavenly peace on earth."

The ceremony in London was organised by The Princess of Wales's Royal Regiment, successor to The Middlesex Regiment, and took place at the Far East Prisoners of War Memorial in Camden. It was attended by representatives of some of the units on board the *Lisbon Maru*, and family members of prisoners of war. Wreaths were laid on behalf of The Middlesex Regiment, The Royal Scots, the Burma Star Association and others, including one on behalf of the *Lisbon Maru* Association of Hong Kong and another for the East China Sea Development Institute. The last known survivor, Dennis Morley of the Royal Scots, was not able to attend the event, but watched it through a video link set up by the grandson of Arthur Betts, one of the prisoners, whom Dennis remembers. Dennis wrote down some thoughts which were read out at the ceremony and it is perhaps fitting that these words should end this part of the book:

"From Dennis Morley, 2nd Battalion, Royal Scots, Date of Birth 26 October 1919.

"I was on the *Lisbon Maru* troop ship carrying Japanese troops and prisoners of war. It was travelling from Hong Kong to Japan. The *Lisbon Maru* was torpedoed off Zhoushan, which was on Chinese territory, by United States Submarine *Grouper*. The Captain didn't know there were POWs on board.

"When the *Lisbon Maru* was sinking we managed to get into the water and started being rescued by some Chinese fishermen. The Japanese eventually started to rescue us too.

"I was picked up by a Japanese boat and was naked and nearly froze to death. I was not given clothes until we reached Shanghai. The Japanese did a head count and it was discovered that 850 POWs had drowned. The remaining POWs were taken on the *Shinsui Maru* ship, to Moji in Japan, and then by train to Kobe and Osaka. I was put in Kobe house and worked as a stevedore in the docks, loading and unloading ships.

"I would like to say a BIG THANK YOU to ALL THE CHINESE FISHERMEN who came to our rescue on that day seventy-five years ago. And THANK YOU to some JAPANESE SOLDIERS who were very kind and gave us green tea, which tasted like nectar, and also cigarettes.

"Since the war and in recent years I have been on a reconciliation trip to Japan, for which I am VERY GRATEFUL and feel honoured to have been given this chance to come to terms with it all. I also attended a Remembrance Day on 11 November a few years ago, and I laid a wreath at a memorial in Hong Kong.

"I have been shown such great kindness from Chinese and Japanese people alike and have made many good friends.

"THANK YOU FOR GIVING ME THE REST OF MY LIFE.

"When I was a POW I never dreamt I would live to be ninety-seven years old.

"ONCE AGAIN, TO ALL OF THOSE PEOPLE INVOLVED, THANK YOU FOR SAVING MY LIFE.

"With my warmest wishes for your future health and happiness and a peaceful life."

The Middlesex Regiment connection

I was commissioned into the Middlesex Regiment in 1960. When I joined the 1st Battalion I was impressed by two of the many pictures hanging in the Officers' Mess. The first was the famous painting by Lady Butler "Steady the Drums and Fifes", showing the 57th of Foot (which later became the Middlesex Regiment) drawn up on the ridge at Albuhera, where their stoicism in the face of a continued onslaught by the enemy earned them the immortal nickname, "The Diehards".

The second was a sketch of the sinking of the *Lisbon Maru* by Lieut WC Johnson, drawn from eye-witness accounts, the same that is featured on the cover of this book and also in the inside pages. Apart from the moving image of people desperately struggling for their lives, this had modern relevance as one of the survivors was currently still serving with the Battalion. By 1960, Maj Frank Waldren was a senior officer. Also, regimental folklore told of the horrors on board the ship and of the calmness and strength of Col "Monkey" Stewart whose inspirational leadership ensured the avoidance of panic and organised the breakout. At the time I was unaware of the rescue by Chinese fishermen.

After the war, the newly formed 1st Battalion was posted back to Hong Kong. This was supposed to be an easy posting, as a reward for the tenacity and "Diehard" spirit they had shown in 1941 during the battle for the defence of Hong Kong. Alas, the posting was far from easy as they were sent to fight in the Korean War. In their wisdom, the War Office sent them there in mid-winter equipped with light weight jungle uniforms. But that is another story...

During their time in Hong Kong, the Battalion kept in touch with Miles "Ginger" Howell – the young officer who had carried out the breakout from the ship's hold with a butcher's knife – who had settled in Hong Kong after the war. In recognition of the fact that he had saved the lives of many members of the Regiment, he was presented with a small gift as a token of appreciation. This was a 57th of Foot cross-belt plate of the kind worn during the Peninsular War, marked with the battle honour, "Albuhera". Howell died in 1966 and his widow returned the cross-belt plate to the Middlesex Regiment as it would mean more to them than to her – she had not known Howell until after the war. She gave it to Capt Gordon Crumley of the Middlesex Regiment who at the time was serving as Adjutant of the Royal Hong Kong Regiment. He in turn offered it to the Middlesex Regimental Museum, but they declined the offer as the Regiment was being amalgamated with others to form The Queen's Regiment and the museum was in the process of closing. Gordon Crumley held on to the cross-belt plate for many years.

Meantime, my career had changed course. Having studied Chinese in the 1960s, I later left the Army and had a second career with the Diplomatic Service, serving for many years in Hong Kong. After retiring, I continued to enjoy links there and came across Nelson Mar and the *Lisbon Maru* Association of Hong Kong. It was therefore relatively recently that I learned of the involvement of the Zhoushan fishermen in the rescue. My interest in the *Lisbon Maru* Incident developed from there, based on my background in The Middlesex Regiment, my contacts in China and Hong Kong, and interest in the Chinese language.

In 2011, I learned that there was a plan for some of the Zhoushan fishermen to visit the UK the following year. As there was no official UK involvement I decided to do what I could to arrange a proper welcome for them. During these preparations, Gordon Crumley gave me the cross-belt plate, originally given to Howell, so that it could be presented to the fishermen. In the event, this visit did not take place, as the fishermen were too old and frail to travel so far. I therefore passed this on to Kent Shum of the *Lisbon Maru* Association of Hong Kong, who in turn sent it to the Dongji Museum of History and Culture, where it is now on display.

Translating from Chinese

There are many challenges in translating from Chinese into English. The first is to understand the nature of Chinese characters. A single character is not (generally) a word as we understand the idea in English, nor does it necessarily have a distinct meaning. It is more a concept, which has a generalised sense of meaning that becomes specific and precise only when taken in context. For example, the character 中 is an ideogram which gives the idea of centre or middle. Depending entirely on the context in which the character is used, it can have any one of the following meanings: *centre, middle, China, in, among, amidst, mid, mean, halfway between two extremes, in the process of, fit for, good for, all right, OK, to hit, to fit exactly, be hit by, fall into, be affected by, suffer*; and probably several more meanings besides.

Context is everything. When this character, 中, is combined with the character for country, 国, this produces the concept of the central – or most important – country, otherwise the Middle Kingdom: 中国, in other words, China. So far, so good, but that is far from the end of the story. For example, the characters for "develop" (发展), when followed by 中, this time meaning, "in the process of", produce the adjective "developing" (发展中). The term for "nation" is 国家 (literally, "country home"), so the expression "developing nations" becomes 发展中国家. The sharp-eyed reader will note that this expression includes the two characters 中国, which, as noted above, normally mean "China". But, of course, here they don't mean "China". This is just a simple illustration of the point that no character or combination of characters has a meaning except in context. And this context is sometimes not limited to the sentence in which the expression is found, but can be influenced by the wider surrounding text. At times during the translation of this book I have looked at a sentence, understood every single character in it, understood the rest of the paragraph, and at first not had a clue as to the meaning of the sentence. Sometimes it took several days until eventually the strands came together and the meaning became clear.

The structure of the Chinese language differs greatly from that of many European languages, including English. In English, we are used to seeing first the subject of a sentence, which helps us understand what is going on. For example, "The man who was sitting on a rock fell into the sea". We immediately know that we are talking about a man and what happened to him. In Chinese, this would be expressed as, "Sitting on rock man fell into sea." Or, if you choose to add the definite and indefinite articles, which don't exist in Chinese, "The sitting on a rock man fell into the sea." In a simple sentence like this, there is no challenge. But many Chinese sentences are extremely long, complex and intertwined.

I will use one sentence from *A Faithful Record* as an illustration and translate it word by word. This process produces the following reading:

Just villagers' General Secretary Zhao Xiaoru and villagers' representative Committee Chairman Tang Pin'gen and Tang Ruliang, Xu Yusong, Li Chaohong, Ren Xincang, Wang Xiangshui, Weng Azhou and so on were discussing sending officer with Dingxiang guerrilla command post Resistance Self Defence Regiment (The 4th Regiment) contact rescue foreign allied soldiers when, Japanese Army five warships already surrounded Dongji all the islands, furthermore, in the afternoon separately many routes began towards Qingbang and Miaozihu two islands targetedly carry out big clean-up; perhaps in order to protect three special statusers and not let island on ordinary people more troubles, living at temple and fishermen's homes inside's foreigners heard comrades' blowing whistles sound all automatically came out assembled, immediately all by Japanese soldiers escorted onto warship.

Yes, I've had to make up a couple of English words to reflect the Chinese terms used.

Once the tortuous structures are unravelled, the sentence is rendered as follows:

Just as the villagers' General Secretary Zhao Xiaoru and Chairman of the villagers' representative Committee Tang Pin'gen and Tang Ruliang, Xu Yusong, Li Chaohong, Ren Xincang, Wang Xiangshui, Weng Azhou and others were discussing sending an officer to contact the Dingxiang guerrilla command post of the Resistance Self Defence Regiment (The 4th Regiment) to rescue the foreign allied soldiers, five Japanese naval warships had surrounded all the Islands of Dongji. Furthermore, in the afternoon they began a targeted clean-up from many different directions of the two islands of Qingbang and Miaozihu. Perhaps in order to protect the three with special status and so as not to add to the troubles of the ordinary people on the islands, when the foreigners living in the temple and the fishermen's homes heard the sound of their comrades blowing whistles, they came out and assembled of their own accord and were immediately escorted onto a warship by the Japanese soldiers.

In this example I have broken the one long sentence into three. In other cases it is often necessary to use several English sentences for one Chinese sentence. Punctuation is still a relatively new feature in written Chinese and its use is not always compatible with practice in the West.

Written Chinese was developed by élite and élitist scholars and officials. Ordinary people were discouraged – some forbidden – from learning to read and write. The written language bore no relation to any spoken language. Although the characters could be pronounced, if a passage of classical Chinese was read aloud to someone who had not been taught to read, he would not be able to make any sense of what he heard. Over the centuries, writing was gradually brought more into line with speech, and today written Chinese is more or less identical to official spoken Mandarin Chinese. Following the spread of literacy and the widespread use of Mandarin as the official language throughout China over the last half century or so, today, a passage read aloud from the *People's Daily* would be readily understood by anyone from most parts of China, even if they were illiterate.

The *lingua franca* in Hong Kong is Cantonese, which is structurally very different to Mandarin, and the two languages are not mutually intelligible. Unlike most of mainland China, Mandarin has not spread to Hong Kong as a normal means of communication. Although these days – especially since Hong Kong reverted to Chinese sovereignty in 1997 – more and more people can understand Mandarin and to a limited extent can use it to communicate with mainlanders, it remains very much a foreign language; but Cantonese continues to dominate. When a

Cantonese person reads a Chinese newspaper, the structure and grammar of the written language – which equates to Mandarin – is different to the language he speaks. One result of this is that writers in Hong Kong, who have no instinctive feel for colloquial Mandarin grammar, tend to be more literary in style. This is true of Hong Kong Chinese-language newspapers and is certainly true of the Chinese-language book, *A Faithful Record of the "Lisbon Maru" Incident.* Much of it is written in this semi-literary style favoured by the Hong Kong Chinese, whereas some later passages, written by mainland reporters, are more colloquial and (for me) easier to understand and therefore to translate.

Another development in the written language has been the simplification of many Chinese characters. For example, the expression quoted earlier, for "developing nations" (发展中国家), contains some simplified characters. If rendered in traditional characters they would look like this: 發展中國家. Simplified characters are used universally in mainland China, but Hong Kong (and the Chinese book *A Faithful Record of the "Lisbon Maru" Incident*) continues to use traditional characters. A library of several different Chinese-English dictionaries is necessary to cope with all but the simplest task of translation; I have a couple of dozen or so, including some Cantonese-English volumes, and during the course of this translation, I needed to refer to many of them. Most are indexed in simplified characters, making it rather awkward and slow to identify unknown traditional characters. And in a book of this length there were of course many characters I did not know. After all, there are some 40,000 Chinese characters altogether, and I would not pretend to know more than a fraction of these.

It is often said that one of the advantages of the Chinese written language is that all Chinese living anywhere in the world – and even Japanese – can understand each other because they use the same characters. Whilst this is largely correct, there are some differences. Cantonese has some unique characters which are unofficial and not formally recognised, but are nonetheless used in certain publications (although not in this volume). For example "有" is the character for, "to have". If the two horizontal strokes in the middle are removed, the result is the Cantonese character for "have not" (my Chinese word-processor can't reproduce this character because it is not recognised). Also there are words in Cantonese that are quite different from those used in Mandarin; for instance in Mandarin the characters for "office" translate as "the room for doing work"; whereas in Cantonese it is "the building for writing"; and this applies even where the office is a single room rather than an office block, which would seem to be implied by the characters.

As well as specific words, there are many cases of differences in style of expression used by the Cantonese, which a Mandarin speaker would not readily understand. Fortunately I can also speak Cantonese and have been able to cope with these nuances, as well as with the names of places and personalities in Hong Kong through having lived in Hong Kong for many years.

The Chinese book, *A Faithful Record of the "Lisbon Maru" Incident* also contains many Japanese names of people or places. This is another difficulty; for, buried in a sentence of Chinese, the characters for a Japanese name appear to be simply another two or three Chinese characters. There is no signpost to say they are Japanese; simply the context shows that it is a Japanese name. Here I have been helped enormously by the power of the internet. By inputting the Chinese characters into a search engine, it was often possible to find an article, referring either to a place, or to a Second World War event in which the Japanese person concerned is mentioned, using both the Chinese characters (or rather the Japanese Kanji, which are the same) and the Romanised version of the name, thus giving me the information that I needed.

I hope that in this translation I have managed to convey both the content and the equally important flavour of the original Chinese work for the benefit of the English reader.

Brian Finch
November 2016

Additional Reading

References

Gillian Bickley. *Hong Kong Invaded: A '97 Nightmare*. Hong Kong: Hong Kong University Press, 2001.
Lt Cdr Henry CS Collingwood-Selby, RN (1898-1992), *In Time Of War*. Richard Collingwood-Selby and Gillian Bickley (Eds). Hong Kong: Proverse Hong Kong, 2013.
Shigeru Mizuki; translated by Zack Davison. *Shōwa 1939-1944: A History of Japan*. USA: Drawn and Quarterly, 3 June 2014.
Hong Kong News. A Japanese wartime publication.
Charles Jordan (oral history). Imperial War Museum Collections Catalogue number 19638.

Internet References

70th Anniversary Commemorations in Dongji.
www.56.com/u68/v_NzQxNDU4NjU.html^
William Arthur Barlow. http://www.jacksdale.org.uk/war-memorial/second-world-war-fallen/barlow-william-arthur
Kobe House.
www.mansell.com/pow_resources/camplists/osaka/kobe/kobehouse-main.htm
Lisbon Maru. Britain at War. www.britain-at-war.org.uk/ww2/Hong_Kong/html/lisbon_maru.htm
Lisbon Maru. POW Research Network, Japan.
www.powresearch.jp/en/archive/ship/lisbon.html
Lisbon Maru. www.fepow-community.org.uk/monthly_revue/html/lisbon_maru.htm
Lisbon Maru. Wikipedia. en.wikipedia.org/wiki/Lisbon_Maru
Scotland/China Articles. www.scotchina.org/index.php/feature-articles
Speech by President Xi Jinping at the State Banquet at Buckingham Palace on 20 October 2016.
www.youtube.com/watch?v=G2p7BI07L_A^
The Fall of Hong Kong: Allied POWs Marching to Shamshuipo 30th December 1941
www.hongkongescape.org/Maltby.htm

The Remarkable Story of Francis McKane.
www.ulsterheritage.com/history/francis_mckane.htm
The Sinking of the Lisbon Maru.
cofepow.org.uk/pages/ships_lisbon_maru.htm
U.S.S Canopus, AS-9. evperry.com/canopus.html
舟山广电海洋宽频网 *(Zhoushan Radio Ocean Broadband Net)*
www.wifizs.cn/folder1/folder127/2015-10-21/37903.html^
Tony Banham. *Roll of Honour: Lisbon Maru*. Britain at War.
www.roll-of-honour.org.uk/Hell_Ships/Lisbon_Maru
Douglas Bridgewater. *Heroes of Henley: Thomas Ritchings Gunner, 872724, Royal Artillery (1920-1942)*. Henley News On-Line. www.henleynews.co.uk/07_05_17.html
Brian Finch. *Walk for War Heroes.*
bfinch.wix.com/walkforwarheroes and
walkforwarheroes.yolasite.com
L/Cpl James Gow. *"Lisbon Maru": Martyrs of the East.*
www.fepow-day.org/html/lisbon_maru.htm
Vic.Ient *The Ient Family: Family History: The Sinking of the Lisbon Maru.*
www.ient.org.uk/index.php?page=the-sinking-of-the-lisbon-maru
Val Kvalheim. *"Submarine Sagas": The Sinking of the "Lisbon Maru"*. Polaris, February 1995.
www.subvetpaul.com/SAGA_2_95.htm
Arthur Lane. *The Sinking of the Lisbon Maru, 1 October 1942.*
www.fepow-community.org.uk/arthur_lane/html/sinking_of_the_lisbon_maru.htm
James McHarg Miller. *Lisbon Maru.* www.far-eastern-heroes.org.uk/james_mcharg_miller/html/lisbon_maru_1.htm
Desmond Wettern, Collection. *The Battle of Hong Kong 1941.*
www.iwm.org.uk/collections/search?query=IWM+HU2779%2C&=Search&items_per_page=10

Key to Symbols

^ Chinese language websites
* websites no longer valid
# links leading to the home page of Chinese websites, not to any specific article

Some useful image sources

Cognitio Sapiens Ngensis. www.ngensis.com/jap7/jap07-1.htm.
flickr: Panzer DB Type 89 A I-Go Kō (Chi-Ro).
www.flickr.com/photos/deckarudo/6302204318
*Homecoming of First British Prisoner of War from Japanese
Prison Camp.* London, United Kingdom. Foreign Office Political
Intelligence Department (PID) Second World War Photograph
Library: Classified Print Collection (photographs.
www.iwm.org.uk/collections/search?query=HU+93201&=Search
&items_per_page=10
Leaving Hong Kong. Getty Images.
www.gettyimages.co.uk/license/3088017
Mare Island Museum. www.mareislandmuseum.org
National Archives. www.nationalarchives.gov.uk/
National Army Museum. https://www.nam.ac.uk/picture-library
*Naval History and Heritage Command: NH 90800 USS
GROUPER (SSK-214).*
www.history.navy.mil/our-collections/photography/numerical-
list-of-images/nhhc-series/nh-series/NH-90000/NH-90800.html
NavSource Online: Submarine Photo Archive.
www.navsource.org/archives/08/08214.htm
NYK (Nippon Yusen Kaisha) Maritime Museum.
www.nyk.com/rekishi/e/
Imperial War Museum.
http://www.iwm.org.uk/collections/photographs
Pet Love Shack:.U.S. Submarine GROUPER -214.
www.petloveshack.com/GrouperSubmarine.html
Ships of the U.S. Navy, 1940-1945: SS-214 USS Grouper.
www.ibiblio.org/hyperwar/USN/ships/SS/SS-214_Grouper.html
Bob Hackett. *RIKUGUN-SEN: Stories and Battle Histories of
Selected Imperial Army Vessels.*
www.combinedfleet.com/Rikugun-sen.htm
Dave Paul. *USS GROUPER (SS-214) (SSK-214) (AGSS-214).*
Navy Veterans. navyvets.com/group/ussgrouperss214agss214

Notes

All the notes below are provided by the translator and do not form part of the original Chinese book.

[1] This table lists the contents of this translation, which shows where the translation begins and ends. Within the translation, on p. 24 is the translation of the original table of contents in the Chinese book, which details the various chapters and sections.

[2] The captions to the illustrations are all direct translations from the original Chinese captions, except for the image of Qingbang Island, where the original caption is given in an endnote and similarly for the captions to the two images of the *Lisbon Maru* on pp. 40 and 41. In some cases illustration attributions have been added that were not in the original Chinese captions.

[3] Although the caption to the picture says he took part in the rescue, this is not strictly accurate. He was not a fisherman but, as explained in detail in the text, he was second-in-command of the local anti-Japanese resistance unit and played a key role in helping to arrange the escape of the three prisoners

[4] Although the caption to the picture says that she fed the survivors, her role was more significant. Many of the villagers fed the survivors, but Weng was one of a very few who fed the three escaped prisoners who had been hidden in a cave.

[5] In the original Chinese book, this section appears on pp. 10-11 inclusive.

[6] In the original Chinese book, this section appears on pp. 12-13 inclusive. The speech in English appears on p. 13 of the original Chinese book with a Chinese translation on p. 12. It was given on 16 June 2005 at the welcoming dinner for the visiting fishermen from Zhoushan. (Information provided by the *Lisbon Maru* Association of Hong Kong.)

[7] This is a translation of the original table of contents in the Chinese book, *A Faithful Record of the "Lisbon Maru" Incident* and lists only the material that was in the Chinese book. All other material is shown in the main Table of Contents above.

[8] 1816: the correct number is 1,834. See 'Statistics' in the Additional Material.

[9] In the original Chinese book, this section appears on pp. 16-48 inclusive. This is the main part of the book, and describes the background to the Japanese invasion and occupation of China, the battle for Hong Kong, the plight of the prisoners of war (POWs), the

sailing of the *Lisbon Maru* with POWs on board, the torpedo attack, the sinking, the shooting of prisoners by the Japanese, the rescue by the Chinese fishermen, the hiding and subsequent escape of three of the British POWs and the eventual fate of those who had survived the sinking. The information was compiled by members of the *Lisbon Maru* Association of Hong Kong under the direction of the then Chairman, the late Nelson Mar, BEM, edited by the publishers SoftRepublic and published on 25 July 2007. (Information provided by the *Lisbon Maru* Association of Hong Kong.)

[10] Johnson was a US naval officer, not a British soldier. See following note.

[11] The writing on the sketch says "DRAWN IN KOBE, JAPAN, BY W. C. JOHNSON LIEUT (SC) U.S. NAVY FOR THE OFFICIAL RECORDS OF THE MIDDLESEX REGIMENT ~", and "SINKING OF THE "LISBON MARU" IN THE CHINA SEA, 2 OCTOBER, 1942 AS A RESULT OF TORPEDOING. 1ST BATTALION, MIDDLESEX REGT ABOARD AS PRISONERS OF WAR." Johnson served on the submarine USS *Canopus* and was taken prisoner at Corregidor in the Philippines. He later drew this sketch, from eye-witness accounts, in Osaka #2 Branch POW camp, known as Kobe, or "Kobe House" camp, formerly a warehouse used by Butterfield and Swire. Although no information is available to identify these eye-witnesses, it is likely that they would have been some of the many *Lisbon Maru* survivors who were incarcerated there. The drawing was kept for over two years rolled inside a bamboo stick by Maj CMM Man MC, 1st Battalion The Middlesex Regiment. The sketch is surmounted by the cap badge worn by members of the Middlesex Regiment during and after World War Two. The Middlesex Regimental Museum no longer exists; the original sketch is now held in the National Army Museum in Chelsea. At least one other version of this sketch exists, surmounted by the cap badge of the Royal Scots, who were also among the prisoners of war on the *Lisbon Maru*.

[12] The Chinese characters used here (and throughout the book) are pronounced Qingbin; but the correct characters are pronounced Qingbang, which is the correct name for the Island.

[13] 1,816: the correct number is 1,834. See section on Statistics.

[14] 843: the correct number is 828.

[15] The Chinese word used was the generic term for "buried". But since the wreck of the *Lisbon Maru* can be regarded as a tomb, "entombed" seems more appropriate.

[16] The last Emperor of China.

[17] According to Tony Banham the Compulsory Service Ordinance was passed in June 1939.

[18] Handwriting on the photograph notes that this was taken two days before they left for overseas.

[19] His appointment was as Commander British Troops in China.

[20] It was actually 18 kilometres long.

[21] According to Tony Banham there were seven infantry companies in the Hong Kong Volunteer Defence Corps .

[22] There were no Australian units in Hong Kong.

[23] Now Tuvalu.

[24] According to figures supplied by Tony Banham (*The Sinking of the "Lisbon Maru": Britain's Forgotten Wartime Tragedy*, p. 38) 1,865 paraded to board the *Lisbon Maru*. Later some of the seriously ill were sent back to camp and 1,834 remained on board when the ship sailed.

[25] The original Chinese caption to these two images said "The *Lisbon Maru* was originally owned by the Japanese joint stock company Nippon Yusen Kabushiki-Kaisha, one of thousands of merchant vessels commandeered by the Japanese military for the war."

[26] Tony Banham's figures (*ibid*, p. 41) suggest hold number one held 362, as seventeen had transferred themselves to hold number two; 380 were allocated to hold number three, but some were put into hold number two, which had 1,075 plus the extras from the other holds, making a total of 1,834 on board.

[27] The *Grouper* formally entered service with the US Navy in February 1942. With a submerged displacement of 2,424 tons, it had ten torpedo tubes (six fore and four aft), twenty-four torpedos, a 3-inch gun, a .50-inch machine-gun and a .30-inch anti-aircraft machine-gun. And at that time, like all submarines, the *Grouper* was designed along the lines of traditional ships. Its surface sailing power was good compared to its submerged sailing power. The *Grouper*, which sank four enemy ships in wartime, having been through the Second World War, remained in service with the US Navy until it was retired in 1968.

[28] According to Tony Banham (*The Sinking of the "Lisbon Maru": Britain's Forgotten Wartime Tragedy*, p. 66), the torpedo struck the propeller part of the starboard stern.

[29] According to Tony Banham's account *(ibid*, p. 67), the sixth torpedo did not hit the *Lisbon Maru* although it did explode, perhaps as a result of a shell fired from the ship's guns.

[30] The English language labels were translated by the translator and inserted into the image.

[31] The sinking of the *Lisbon Maru*, at 08.55 on the morning of 2 October 1942, taken from the *Toyokuni Maru*, while the *Kohu Maru No 1* takes off the final crew members from the starboard stern of the vessel.

[32] Tony Banham's account says that Lt Potter was mortally wounded but did not die immediately. Howell took him back to the hold before he died. (See *The Sinking of the "Lisbon Maru": Britain's Forgotten Wartime Tragedy*, p. 82.)

[33] Distinct from a life jacket, a life belt is an inflatable device worn around the waist like a belt to provide buoyancy

[34] The English language labels have been translated and inserted into the image.

[35] Xifushan is the island next to Qingbang Island, marked on the aerial photograph above.

[36] This clearly should read "all three islands". It seems as if somehow the Qingbang islanders hardly recognise Xifushan as a different island.

[37] A temple dedicated to Tian Hou (Tin Hau in Cantonese), Empress of Heaven, Goddess of the Sea and the patron of Chinese fishermen. Such a temple is an important feature of every Chinese fishing village.

[38] This figure does not seem to tie in with the figures in the following paragraph, nor do those add up to 635, but these are the figures used in the Chinese book.

[39] It is not clear which unit this refers to.

[40] The identity of this individual is not entirely clear. The original Chinese text gives Lt Kebosen (the transliteration of an English name). The most likely candidate would seem to be Capt Norman Cuthbertson, Royal Scots, who (according to the lists in Tony Banham's book *We Shall Suffer There*, p. 100) died in Osaka # 2 Branch Camp (Kobe) on 17 October 1942, four days before Lt Col "Monkey" Stewart.

[41] According to Tony Banham, a total of 245 *Lisbon Maru* survivors died in captivity before the end of the war, not all in the first year. (*The Sinking of the "Lisbon Maru": Britain's Forgotten Wartime Tragedy*, Appendix 3.)

[42] 1,816: the correct number is 1,834. See section on Statistics.

[43] 843: the correct number is 828.

[44] 244: the correct number is 245.

[45] 1,092: the correct number is 1,073.

[46] 724: the correct number is 761.

[47] Although the Chinese says gunfire (i.e. fire from artillery or ships' guns) the Japanese were using rifles and machine-guns.

[48] In the original Chinese book, this section appears on pp. 50-58 inclusive. It describes the visit to Zhoushan by former POW and *Lisbon Maru* survivor Mr Charles Jordan and family and was written immediately after the visit. This report, by a reporter who accompanied the Jordan family on the sea journey to Dongji Island during the visit to Zhoushan, was originally published in the *Zhoushan Daily* on 18 August 2005. (Information provided by the *Lisbon Maru* Association of Hong Kong.)

[49] The name "Dongji" means "extreme east".

[50] No Australian units were stationed in Hong Kong at the time.

[51] There were no Australians on board the *Lisbon Maru.*

[52] The text says 1942, but he must mean 1945.

[53] The text says 2006, but presumably this should be 2005.

[54] There were no Australians on board the *Lisbon Maru.*

[55] King George VI of course.

[56] After being recaptured by the Japanese, Charles Jordan was taken by ship to Moji and was put in hospital along with thirty to forty others. He was one of only nine or ten to survive and after about a week was sent by train to one of several prisoner-of-war camps in Osaka. He and his colleagues were put to work in the dockyards working as stevedores carrying 85 kilogramme sacks. At the end of the war he returned home via Pearl Harbour, Canada, New York and finally on board the Queen Mary to Southampton. This information came from his oral account recorded by the Imperial War Museum, 'Charles Jordan, (Oral history)', catalogue number 19638. Richard Jordan has described his life back home in the UK after the war, when he turned his hand to a variety of jobs to support his family of a wife, two sons and three daughters, including as a night telephonist with the GPO, and working for Surrey County Council in delivering school meals and later as a groundsman.

[57] In the original Chinese book, this section appears on pp. 59-63 inclusive. It is an account by a reporter following an interview with Mr Jordan on 18 August 2007 and was published on the Zhoushan website *Zhoushan Net* at the request of Kent Shum, Secretary of the *Lisbon Maru* Association. (Information provided by the *Lisbon Maru* Association of Hong Kong.)

[58] 1,816: the correct number is 1,834. See section on Statistics.

[59] During a business trip to Zhoushan, Wang Yongjian, a trader, met and recognised Miao Zhifen. She told him the story of her father's key role in helping the escape and transfer to Chongqing of the three POWs Evans, Fallace and Johnstone. Wang compiled this written account from
Miao's oral recollection and gave it to Kent Shum, Secretary of the *Lisbon Maru* Association of Hong Kong when Kent Shum visited Zhoushan in April 2007. (Information provided by the *Lisbon Maru* Association of Hong Kong.)

[60] This note is in the original Chinese text.

[61] The text says "Little Bay Cave", but this would seem to be a misprint for Child Cave.

[62] Weng is pictured in a photograph a few pages below.

[63] The words in square brackets were not in the original Chinese text but were implied from the context.

[64] Curiously, the last character in Miao Kaiyun's name used here (運)is different to that used in the caption to the photo above (蕓), although it is clearly the same person.

[65] The text says "Little Bay Cave", but this would seem to be a misprint for Child Cave.

[66] "The War of Resistance against Japan" is the usual Chinese term for what the West calls the Pacific Campaign in the Second World War.

[67] Both Johnstone and Fallace were WOs in the Hong Kong Royal Naval Volunteer Reserve; Fallace joined the Royal Indian Navy only after the war.

[68] This is the same person as the Yang Fu referred to on p. 57.

[69] This note is in the original Chinese text.

[70] Tony Banham, author of *The sinking of the "Lisbon Maru": Britain's Forgotten Wartime Tragedy*, who undertook extensive research before publishing that book, is adamant that there were no families on board the *Lisbon Maru*. Perhaps whatever it was that Evans said was misunderstood due to language difficulties.

[71] The significance of the "Scotland the Brave" tea towel might not be immediately obvious. Perhaps it was presented to Miss Miao by Sophia Anne Foley and her younger sister Maureen Helen Donald, who accompanied Charles Jordan on his visit to Zhoushan and two of whose uncles served with the Royal Scots and died in the *Lisbon Maru* Incident.

[72] This note is in the original Chinese text.

[73] A Buddhist nunnery.

[74] A small town near Ningbo.

[75] No further details are known about this article or the author.

[76] Some died in captivity and did not make it home.

[77] In the original Chinese book, this section appears on pp. 73-74 inclusive. These vignettes on memorabilia were reported in an article on the Zhejiang provincial web-based news channel. The date of the report is not known. (Information was provided by the *Lisbon Maru* Association of Hong Kong.*)*

[78] JNW9375 is the gold mark: maker: JNW, 9 carat gold, 375 fineness. The initials on the ring are JG. When villagers from Zhoushan visited Hong Kong in July 2005 they showed this ring to Tony Banham and asked if he was able to identify the owner so that it could be returned. He was unable to do so.

[79] In the original Chinese book, this section appears on pp. 75-94 inclusive. A group of Hong Kong students accompanied Mr Jordan on his visit to Zhoushan as part of a programme to learn history "by exposure" rather than just through books. The following five accounts were written by the students immediately afterwards. The first writer was studying in the UK at the time of the visit and also acted as interpreter for Mr Jordan and the others. (Information provided by the *Lisbon Maru* Association of Hong Kong.)

[80] Sophia Anne Foley and her younger sister Maureen Helen Donald. Their uncles served with the Royal Scots and died in the shipwreck. (Information provided by Kent Shum, Secretary of the *Lisbon Maru* Association of Hong Kong.)

[81] Mr Jordan was of course the only member of the party to be visiting the site again.

[82] This clearly refers to the others in the party, not Mr Jordan himself.

[83] 1,816: the correct number is 1,834. See section on Statistics.

[84] Although surprised by Charles Jordan's actions, the fisherman happily joined in and expressed his feelings in the same way.

[85] Shamshuipo was used as a prisoner-of-war camp during the War.

[86] The traditional Chinese calendar is technically a lunisolar calendar but is often referred to as a lunar calendar.

[87] 843: the correct number is 828. See section on Statistics.

[88] The Chinese Dongji means "extreme east"

[89] The students who took part in this visit to Zhoushan did so as part of a course in practical Second World War History.

[90] Some poetic licence here!

[91] Kent Shum, Secretary of the *Lisbon Maru* Association of Hong Kong. It is common practice in Chinese to refer to a person in authority by their title, followed by their surname, hence "Guide Shum".

[92] Typhoon Matsa, referred to in an earlier section.

[93] In the original Chinese book, this section appears on pp. 95-96 inclusive. Chen Yafang and Ni Ligang reported on the reaction of the Hong Kong students to Mr Jordan's visit to Zhoushan. The report was published in the local newspaper, the *Zhoushan Daily*, on 18 August 2005. (Information provided by the *Lisbon Maru* Association of Hong Kong.)

[94] In the original Chinese book, this section appears on pp. 97-99 inclusive. In June 2005 five elderly fishermen from Zhoushan who had helped in the 1942 rescue of British POWs flew to Hong Kong where they were welcomed and thanked for their courage. This account by reporters who accompanied the Zhoushan fishermen on their visit to Hong Kong was published in the *Zhoushan Daily* in June 2005. This information was provided by the *Lisbon Maru* Association of Hong Kong.

[95] 1,816: the correct number is 1,834. See the section on Statistics.

[96] Front centre is Mr Maximo Cheng, President of the Hong Kong Second World War Veterans' Association. On the other side of Brigadier Hammerbeck is Dr Tony Banham, author of *The Sinking of the "Lisbon Maru": Britain's Forgotten Wartime Tragedy*. Apart from the elderly fishermen, the others in the picture are officials from Zhoushan.

[97] The placard reads, "Grieve. Deep condolences for the British soldiers who died in the disaster of the sinking of the *Lisbon Maru* from the Zhoushan City visiting delegation of elderly fishermen".

[98] In the original Chinese book, this section appears on pp. 100-102 inclusive. This is a separate article by Chen Yafang reporting on specific aspects of the fishermen's visit to Hong Kong, published in the *Zhoushan Daily* in June 2005. (Information provided by the *Lisbon Maru* Association of Hong Kong.)

[99] 1,816: the correct number is 1,834. See section on Statistics.

[100] The Chinese text says, "Hong Kong stars, representing…" I have put "Hong Kong film stars…" for clarity. The underwater team was hoping to take part in a planned dive to the wreck of the *Lisbon Maru*, but this does not seem to have taken place. The picture also shows the late Nelson Mar, BEM, who was Chairman of the *Lisbon Maru* Association of Hong Kong at the time (centre rear standing between the two actresses) and Dr Tony Banham, author of *The Sinking of the "Lisbon Maru": Britain's Forgotten Wartime Tragedy*, the tallest person standing at the back on the right.

[101] In the original Chinese book, this section appears on pp. 103-107 inclusive. Two reporters, Xie Guoping and Shen Feilun, both from the

Zhejiang provincial newspaper *Zhejiang Daily*, produced this report following research into documentary background. The report was published in 2002 and was found on the website by the *Lisbon Maru* Association of Hong Kong. (Information provided by the *Lisbon Maru* Association of Hong Kong.)

[102] This is a common Chinese term to describe westerners, including those who don't match this physical description.

[103] This would seem to be the ring pictured above in the chapter, 'Tales of *Lisbon Maru* Memorabilia'.

[104] Fallace was one of the three prisoners of war whom the Chinese helped to escape. He joined the Indian Navy after the war.

[105] The original caption in the Chinese book read, "A small wartime episode lies buried in this tiny tranquil fishing village, far from the mainland.". The name of the village does not appear in the Chinese book, but was provided to the translator by the *Lisbon Maru* Association of Hong Kong.

[106] The reporters seem to have made a mistake here; this should be Xifushan. As shown in the map, 'The site of the sinking of the *Lisbon Maru*', above, the four islands include Xifushan, not Dongfushan, which is a larger island off that map further to the southeast. Xi and Dong mean West and East respectively.

[107] In the original Chinese book, this section appears on pp. 108-110 inclusive. This report by Li Min, a reporter from the Zhejiang provincial web-based news channel, was published in 2002 and was found on the website by the *Lisbon Maru* Association of Hong Kong. (Information provided by the *Lisbon Maru* Association of Hong Kong.)

[108] i.e. 1 October1949.

[109] A famous Song dynasty authoress and poet.

[110] This would seem to be the same person as the Lin Fuyun referred to in the next paragraph and elsewhere in this book and may simply be a misprint. To add to the confusion, the only similar name in, 'List of Residents ... who rescued British prisoners of war', is Lin Fuyin.

[111] In the original Chinese book, this section appears on pp. 111-118 inclusive. Zhang Xueqin and Shen Guan, reporters for the provincial newspaper *Zhejiang Daily*, researched previously unpublished documents from the Zhejiang provincial archives and the Zhoushan archives to produce this article and also met Tony Banham to gather information that he had gleaned from some of the survivors of the tragedy. The report was published in 2002 and was found on the website by the *Lisbon Maru* Association of Hong Kong. (Information provided by the *Lisbon Maru* Association of Hong Kong.)

[112] This was the name at that time for Qingbang Island.

[113] The name of the ship is unclear. In Chinese it is pronounced Maikaosi.

[114] An earlier passage in the book says that the fishing households on Qingbang Island were mobilised by the five men Zhao Xiaoru, Tang Pin'gen, Weng Azhou, Tang Ruliang and Xu Yusong.

[115] This group is also described earlier in the book: Shen Wanshou, Wu Qisheng, Lü Deren, Shen Yuanxing and Shen Aming

[116] "Reform and opening-up to the outside world" was both a slogan and a political drive in the 1980s, to further the economic reforms of the then
Chinese leader Deng Xiaoping, which laid the groundwork for China's economic success in recent decades.

[117] 1816: the correct number is 1,834. See the section on Statistics.

[118] Tony Banham is adamant that there were no families on board the *Lisbon Maru* and cannot shed any light on this remark.

[119] This is not accurate. Tony Banham explains that the hatch was opened, some of the prisoners managed to escape, but then the ladder broke and the majority of the prisoners perished when the ship went down. (See, *The Sinking of the "Lisbon Maru": Britain's Forgotten Wartime Tragedy*, pp. 80-81.)

[120] This was 2Lt Geoffrey Hamilton, Royal Scots.

[121] 840: the correct number is 828. See the section on Statistics.

[122] In the original Chinese book, this section appears on pp. 120-122 inclusive.

[123] The text says 8 December. This should be 18 December.

[124] 1,816: the correct number is 1,865. See section on Statistics.

[125] 1,816: the correct number is 1,834.

[126] Most, not all. A few managed to escape before the ladder broke.
(See, *The Sinking of the "Lisbon Maru": Britain's Forgotten Wartime Tragedy*, pp. 80-81.)

[127] In the original Chinese book, this section appears on p.123. The origin of this map is unknown. The Chinese place names and other details have been translated and the English versions inserted.

[128] In the original Chinese book, this section appears on pp. 124-126 inclusive. The section was provided by SoftRepublic in May 2007. SoftRepublic are no longer in business. The original source for this material is unknown. (Information provided by the *Lisbon Maru* Association of Hong Kong.)

[129] The article seems to be saying that the diesel engines, which work only on the surface because of the need for an air intake, as well as driving the engines to propel the submarine, also charge the batteries which run an electric motor that powers the submarine when

submerged. And because battery technology was in its infancy, underwater performance was poor.

[130]This should clearly be "ten" (as described in the third paragraph in this article).

[131] In the original Chinese book, this section appears on pp. 127-129 inclusive. This section was provided by SoftRepublic in May 2007. SoftRepublic are no longer in business The original source for this material is unknown. (Information provided by the *Lisbon Maru* Association of Hong Kong.)

[132] In the original Chinese book, this section appears on pp. 130-131 inclusive. These details were provided by Zhoushan government officials in June 2005 when they accompanied the Zhoushan fishermen on their visit to Hong Kong. (Information provided by the *Lisbon Maru* Association of Hong Kong.) The list is not in alphabetical order nor the Chinese equivalent. The reason for the order of the names is unclear.

[133] In the original Chinese book, this section appears on pp.132-166 inclusive. Tony Banham supplied this original list in English and it was copied by the *Lisbon Maru* Association of Hong Kong from the website: https://www.cofepow.org.uk/hell-ships-casualties-list/lisbon-maru. In the Chinese book the names were printed in English and the Regiment or Corps and Unit were transcribed into Chinese.

[134] In the Chinese book, *A Faithful Record of the" Lisbon Maru" Incident* the second named John Barnes was incorrectly named as also being in the Royal Scots. I have changed this entry by reference to the original Roll of Honour published in English, showing him as a gunner.

[135] In the original Chinese book, this section appears on pp. 167-171 inclusive.

[136] Also at www.canadaatwar.ca/index.php?page=Page&action=showpage&id=32.

[137] This links to an unrelated tourist website for Lisbon in Portugal.

[138] This document is from the National Archives, Kew, under reference WO343, Fiche 214, pp. 38 and 39. From the context it would seem that the account was written by Evans although there is no signature or other confirmation of this and no date. The system of rendering names of people and places into Romanisation at that time is largely unrecognisable today. Many of the place names and personal names are not therefore readily identifiable, but some can be transcribed into pinyin:

Qingbang Island (given here as Tsing-Pan), Zhoushan (Chusan) Archipelago, Hulu (Wooloo) Island, Guoju (Kuochu), General Wang Jineng (Wong Kyi Nun), Wenzhou (Wenchow), Guilin (Kweilin),

Chongqing (Chungking), Zhejiang Province (Chekiang) and Shaoguan, the modern name for Kukong.

[139] The English language version can be found at the following link: https://
news.cgtn.com/news/7859544d79597a6333566d54/share_p.html

Index

FIND OUT MORE ABOUT OUR AUTHORS,
BOOKS, EVENTS AND LITERARY PRIZES

Visit our website: http://www.proversepublishing.com

Visit our distributor's website: <www.chineseupress.com>

Follow us on Twitter
Follow news and conversation: twitter.com/Proversebooks>
OR
Copy and paste the following to your browser window and follow the
instructions: https://twitter.com/#!/ProverseBooks

"Like" us on www.facebook.com/ProversePress

Request our free E-Newsletter
Send your request to info@proversepublishing.com.

Availability
Most titles are available in Hong Kong and world-wide
from our Hong Kong based Distributor, The Chinese University of
Hong Kong Press, The Chinese University of Hong Kong,
Shatin, NT, Hong Kong SAR, China.
Email: cup-bus@cuhk.edu.hk
Website: <www.chineseupress.com>.

All titles are available from Proverse Hong Kong,
http://www.proversepublishing.com
and the Proverse Hong Kong UK-based Distributor.

Stock-holding retailers
Hong Kong (Growhouse, Bookazine)
Singapore (Select Books),
Canada (Elizabeth Campbell Books),
Andorra (Llibreria La Puça, La Llibreria).

Orders from bookshops in the UK and elsewhere.

Ebooks
Many of our titles are available also as Ebooks.

CPSIA information can be obtained
at www.ICGtesting.com
Printed in the USA
LVHW02s1711141117
556257LV00014B/1471/P